The ABC of SEO

Search Engine Optimization Strategies

David George

First edition: March 2005

Lulu Press (www.lulu.com). Lulu ID 102458

ISBN 1-4116-2251-0

Acknowledgements

Thank you to the contributors of the forums: alt.internet.search-engines, Webmaster World and SEO Chat who have exchanged many useful ideas. Will Spencer's Internet Search Engine's FAQ and the Search Engine Watch provided useful information.

Author Bio

David George has been using the Internet since 1987 when he was a Unix Kernel developer, first at Siemens AG then at the Open Software Foundation. He has worked for management consultants McKinsey & Company and Accenture. He helped develop the *talk21.com*, *oneswoop.com* and award winning *capeasi.com* websites. He currently lives in France where he has been working for Reuters and on an OS based project for the French Education Ministry.

By the Same Author

Go Web! Dynamic Web Publishing on the PC Platform; ITP New Media; ISBN: 1-8503-2251-1

Cover Designer: Adrian George

Editor: Geraldine Gadbin

Website: www.abcseo.com

Contents

The ABC of SEO (Search Engine Optimization)

Introduction

I don't know about you but I have got a stack of technical books sitting on my shelves. Guides, Teach Yourselves, How-tos, more literature than my local public library. They are all useful, especially as reference but I doubt I have read more than a fifth of the pages. Normally it is just the introduction and a few chapters to get up to speed on the subject. Paradoxically I have loads of books on all sorts of Internet related subjects when the emergence of the World Wide Web was supposed to do away with dead tree publishing.

Still there is something convenient in being able to grab a book or printout to take on a flight or train journey. Unlike a laptop or palm pilot they are robust and don't tend to get stolen. At least not the tomes I normally read. They are also functional, easy to scan and randomly dip into. How long do we normally get to sit down with a book? Maybe a couple of hours in the day snatched on the commute into the office or once the kids are put to bed. For that you don't want a 500 page doorstop complete with listings, code samples and interactive CD-ROM - all for the great value of $32.79 saving you $7.99 on the normal Amazon retail price. What you need is a concise guide you can read in a few days. The kind of things that the propeller heads at consultancy firms put together for the suits so they can understand and talk with authority on a subject.

The world of Search Engine Optimization is fast changing. Complicated recipes for SEO success are bound to go out of date quicker than those for Tofu. What is needed is a broad understanding of the issues and techniques and a set of tools for analyzing strategies. After that, any reader wanting to know the current state of the art is best served by discussion forums, web resources and magazines. Re-heating a 12 month old dish is not the best formula for success and might actually be counterproductive, a bit like a case of SEO food poisoning! After a brief introduction this book is arranged as an A to Z, it is its own glossary and serves up the topics in bite size chunks with no preference to current importance in SEO thinking.

What is a Search Engine?

From a user standpoint a search engine is a web page that allows keywords or phrases to be entered and returns results based on the relevance of the documents it holds in its index. Relevance is determined by a set of automated routines referred to as algorithms. Search engines index many billions of pages of Internet content ranging from web pages, images, Adobe Portable Document Format (PDF) and Microsoft Word documents through to music and video clips. It would be impossible for a search engine to explore all the data it indexes in real time. Instead it runs a number of automated programs called robots (also called bots, crawlers or spiders). These programs explore the content referenced by in the search engine's index. Starting from the home page of a website and by following the links it finds, a robot can eventually explore all the linked pages in the site and even discover new websites through outbound links. This process is called spidering. Each document that the robot discovers is ranked based on the search engine's algorithms. This provides a concise picture of the content of the page and it is this information that is used when a search is performed.

The search engine builds up its index either by having webmasters submit their sites directly via free or paid submission pages or through discovering new sites during the spidering process described above. Obviously if a search engine doesn't know about a page it won't be found by its users. Yahoo! say that they index around 80% of the Web although it is difficult to know how accurate this statement is. Google claims to have over 8 billion pages in their index. In order to keep the index fresh robots must periodically revisit a site. The amount of time between visits depends on the resources available to the search engine and how up-to-date the search engine wants to keep a particular page. Some of these periodic visits, such as those prior to the Googledance, generate much excitement from search engine experts.

Examples of general purpose Internet search engines are Google, Yahoo! and MSN Search. Most search engines offer advanced search options that allow users to narrow down their search criteria, for example to find recently updated web pages or pages in a certain language. Some popular search engines use indexes from other engines, at the time of writing AOL search is powered by Google's technology. There are also a number of specialty search engines, an example being Google News which indexes news stories from around the world. Google is currently the most popular internet search engine. Users perform over 200 million searches per day on Google and it is estimated that it handles between a half and three quarters of all searches.

What is Search Engine Optimization?

The expression "*Search Engine Optimization*" is something of a misnomer as it is not the Search Engine that is being optimized. The phase describes the process of designing or modifying a website in order to achieve high rankings in search engines results pages (SERPS). Search engine companies would say that web designers should simply get on with producing excellent content and making their sites easy to navigate and let the search engines get on with indexing the resulting pages. On the other hand it can be argued that the search engine algorithm designers have the best idea of what elements constitute a well designed website and by learning from their ideas we should be able to build better websites.

An example would be the infamous *click here* link. Ten years after the Web entered the mainstream web authors are still using this or similar semantically challenged terms. Google, who originated the idea of ranking sites based on links, puts value on the text used in those links. Recognizing this, web designers wanting to achieve high rankings in Google will strive to use meaningful anchor text and increase the hyper-linking of their sites. So long as this isn't taken to extremes, which in any event Google could recognize and ignore or punish, this should improve the user experience.

Optimizing a website requires some knowledge of what factors search engines use when ranking a page and how significant each of these factors is for a particular search engine. Search engines use a mixture of on-page and off-page factors. On-page factors include the obvious such as keyword density but may also include less obvious ones like the ALT text field used in HTML image elements. Off-page factors include the number of inbound or backlinks to the website. Different search engines put different weight on each of these factors; the exact algorithms used are a closely guarded secret and change frequently. SEO experts spend a lot of time analyzing how important each of these is to a particular search engine. If all search engines were perfect then they would all return the most relevant results in the same order. However we are some way from this situation so designing a site that ranks well with all search engines is difficult. SEO experts will also base their decisions on the popularity of a particular search engine. At present this often means designing for Google and perhaps Yahoo! and MSN Search. Where this is done judiciously the optimizations should not exclude high rankings with other search engines.

Enter the Black Hats

People have different reasons for wanting to achieve high rankings but probably the strongest motivation for the majority of sites employing search engine optimization techniques is money. Some website operators say that the end justifies the means. Some of these sites are content poor; a user is sucked in like a spider down a plug-hole with the sole objective of attracting the maximum number of eyeballs to the page. The site may simply be a front for affiliate advertising. The site owner hopes that a certain percentage of visitors will find some of the adverts interesting enough to click on them and so earn him money. Website operators will employ whatever optimizations are necessary in order to attract visitors. These techniques are often referred to as Black Hat SEO. This phrase is drawn from the computer security industry (and ultimately from Westerns) where black hats are the bad guys and white hats the good guys. Black Hat SEO may use tricks including Link Farms and Blog Spamming. Black Hat SEO can be thought of as any technique that gets your website a higher rank in search engine results pages than its content would merit. Black Hat sites often have wildly fluctuating rankings for given keywords as search engines update their algorithms in response to these techniques. The best known of these updates was the Google Florida algorithm change. Black Hat optimizations contravene most search engines' terms and conditions (TOCs) and can get the site banned. For some Black-hatters this is not an issue as they simply establish a new domain and move on but for legitimate businesses with a great deal invested in their web presence it can be nothing short of a disaster.

Search engine optimization and search engine algorithms can be thought of as species in an ecosystem. They are in a constant state of evolution. Some people fear that search engine optimization will eventually lead to results pages that are full of highly optimized but ultimately worthless websites. While in the past search engines have shown their susceptibility to this, particularly from controversial optimizations, it is in the search engine owner's interest to return relevant results. The struggle between search engines and the optimizers should improve the quality of results in the long term.

One thing is certain; doing nothing except producing reams of content is no longer an option. Good website structure and design is a learned process and understanding search engines and how they rank sites is part of that process. The message is simple, optimize or die. Search engine optimization should be an integral part of the site design and not simply considered as an afterthought. Optimization of an established site is certainly possible but can involve a period of upheaval and is certainly more expensive in terms of effort.

Search engine optimization is one place where small websites can really make a difference compared to big business. I've spent over 15 years consulting for some major blue chip outfits and by the time their websites have gone through the mill of management and marketing they are generally a search engine hell of rinky-dinky flashy effects, a triumph of style over substance. Of course the corporates win out by having large advertising budgets to promote their sites in the off-line world. If you are working for a corporate do not despair, the techniques and arguments we'll discuss can help you make a difference.

Search Engine Optimization Firms

Have you had one of those emails in your inbox claiming that they can make your website No.1 for any keywords?

Are you getting the TRAFFIC AND SALES your website deserves?

It goes without saying that if you are not listed in at least the top 20 rankings on the Search Engines, you are missing a HUGE AMOUNT of business!

We specialize in "Search Engine Optimization" -- getting your website ranked high. We will optimize and submit your website to thousands of SEARCH ENGINES and guarantee to get your site rated in the TOP TEN RANKINGS in at least 5 of the following top engines: AltaVista, AOLSearch, Infoseek, MSN, Excite, HotBot, Google, LookSmart, Lycos, WebCrawler, Snap, Northern Light, AskJeeves, CNET, Mamma, and Yahoo. We can provide testimonials from many satisfied customers. We can help you with Keywords Analysis, submission report, ranking report, Hand Submission, HTML optimization and doorway pages.

Getting a high ranking for a popular keyword in a major search engine can be extremely lucrative. This particular email isn't the most extreme example I've come across but two things (apart from the use of capital letters) stand out. They claim to submit the site to thousands of search engines and their techniques include doorway pages which may be considered as spam by some search engines and get the site banned.

Even the promise to rank in the top 20 may be dubious if the chosen keywords are highly competitive. If you are a candidate for paid Search Engine Optimization you should be wary of promises. No-one can guarantee a number one or even a top ten spot for Google or any other search engine for that matter.

Frequently client expectations are unrealistic or just plain naïve and unscrupulous SEO outfits will use Black Hat techniques to ensure a high, but short term rankings. By the time you've realized your mistake, perhaps after a sudden drop in results or even a ban from the major search engines it is too late.

There are good reasons for using an SEO firm, you may not have the time or detailed knowledge to work on your site and be looking for some outside help or you may want an SEO expert to work with and mentor your team during the design process. There are plenty of businesses that can help but before using the services of an SEO firm you should have a basic understanding of the issues especially, what constitutes Black Hat and search engine spam techniques.

There is undoubtedly a lot of skill, experience and knowledge required to perform good Search Engine Optimization. The services an SEO firm or consultant provides may range from general advice about problems with your site to direct edits to your pages. The work may be a one off improvement to an existing site to a long term full-service contract. Hiring consultants to improve an existing site or work with your team during the building of a new site can have excellent paybacks.

Selecting an SEO Firm

Selecting a good SEO firm may come from recommendation but check out the firm's own site to see how highly it ranks in the major search engines; bearing in mind that *search engine optimization* is a very competitive set of keywords. If possible look beyond simple testimonials and ask for case studies. Talk to existing clients and see how their sites rank on the major search engines for their target keywords. It is worth checking in search engine related forums and Google groups to see if the firm has acquired a bad reputation.

The SEO firm should be able to explain the general process they will use to optimize your site. There is a fear from some SEO consultants that they will be giving away trade secrets. It is understandable that they want to protect intellectual property and business processes. However if the firm is being engaged for a large contract, perhaps updating the contents and structure of the whole site, it is not unreasonable to explain the plan in general terms.

Finally clients should remember that the aim of SEO is to improve visits and in the case of commercial sites, to increase profits. While specific rankings in search engines can't be guaranteed the SEO firm should be committed to improving current rankings for relevant search results, agreed in advance with the client and to improve the number of qualified visitors to the site. Increasing traffic by bait and switch techniques such as jump pages will not result in more sales.

How Many Search Engines Are There?

Phil Bradley <http://www.philb.com/webse.htm> had identified around 140 general search engines and says that there are over 2000 search engines in 200 countries. In theory you could submit your site to thousands of search engines. Whether the time spent submitting you site would be worthwhile is questionable:

As an aside, I've never submitted a site I've created to search engine but a random check shows that all the sites are widely listed. This is the power of inbound-links as we will see later.

A Three Cornered Fight

It is important to remember that Search Engine Optimization is a three cornered fight. You are up against the search engines (although it is better to think of it as a partnership) and their rocket scientists who are continually tweaking algorithms and dreaming up new ways of ranking pages and you are in competition with other websites that are targeting the same or overlapping keywords. To be number one you have to not only produce good content but understand how search engines work better than the next guy and put in the effort to use that knowledge.

These factors make your task difficult but at the same time challenging and exciting. There is a certain buzz from researching some new SEO angle, checking out the competition, applying what you have learned then seeing your site bubble up through the rankings. The reward, of course, is more traffic and, if yours is a commercial site, more business.

It is worth reflecting on the objectives of search engines. For publicly listed companies the principal aim is to make money for shareholders. Forget talk about *"not being evil"* and such like, they have a fiducial duty to their owners. From a user perspective if the search engine can return one page at the top of its results that perfectly answers his query it has succeeded. The search engine doesn't have a duty to list commercial sites in its results and where submissions are free it has no contract with websites in its index. If there are a dozen equally relevant pages it only needs to return one of them.

I mention this because I often hear a lot of complaining about how a certain site hasn't been listed, or how it has been dropped from results, especially after some dubious techniques learned from a forum or book have been used. Some people even say they are going to sue the search engine, perhaps by starting a class action with other disgruntled users. Rather than moaning, website owners should find out where they have gone wrong. The aim of an SEO expert is to make sure their pages are among the first few results returned by a search engine for their chosen keywords. The rest of this book will show how search engines work and give ideas on how to go about optimizing a website.

A

Algorithms

An algorithm is a procedure or formula for solving a problem. How do I know that? I went to Google, currently the World's favorite search engine and used the define operator

```
define:Algorithm
```

Google responded with a set of definitions for the term along with the web pages where it found those definitions. But what really happened when I hit Enter? Google certainly didn't scurry off around the World Wide Web looking for that information while I twiddled my thumbs. In fact I didn't get much time for thumb twiddling as the response came back within a second. Instead Google had already searched many billions of web pages carefully sifting through and evaluating their content. Based on my query it was thus able to determine which pages it thought most relevant.

The way that Google sorts pages for relevance is determined by the algorithms it uses. These examine the text in the page, in the instance above the presence of the keyword: *Algorithm* would certainly be pretty important. Continuing with this example the algorithm designer may also guess that definitions occur in alphabetic lists with the keyword starting a paragraph followed by some text giving the definition. This could form the basis of the *definition* search algorithm used by the search engine.

Computers are poor compared to humans at understanding the semantic meaning of web pages and other documents so most search engines also use clues left by humans; the person who wrote the page and people who link to the page. The page author will use tags that are part of the Hypertext Markup Language (HTML) to guide readers. Important topics will begin with a Heading tag; most end users will see this as a larger font. Other web authors may find the content so useful that they link to the page, possibly with relevant anchor text. The search engine can use this information to rank the page compared to others containing the same keywords.

The exact algorithms used by a search engine are a closely guarded secret and evolve with time in order to improve the results offered to users. Search Engine Optimization experts attempt to reverse engineer a search engine's algorithms.

They do this by examining search engine results pages (SERPS), by setting up test pages to observe the results and by exchanging intelligence with other SEO experts on forums or by private contacts. From this information they can infer what factors are significant to a particular search engine. This is done to improve the websites that they are optimizing (white-hat SEO) on the basis that a site that a search engine prefers will also provide a better user experience. Sometimes they find flaws in the mix and implementation of search engine algorithms and they can use this to unfairly improve the rank of their sites over other, possibly more relevant pages (Black Hat SEO). An example would be Google's use of inbound links to rank a page. When Weblogs or Blogs first appeared SEO experts exploited the most popular to write spurious entries in comment fields pointing to the sites they wished to boost. They also set up link farms and secondary sites simply to link, and increase the ranking of their main site. As a result the Google PhDs updated their algorithms to put less weight on this information and even to ban sites using strong Black Hat techniques.

AltaVista

In a time where Google is pre-eminent in the search business it is difficult to conceive how it was otherwise. Once upon a time AltaVista was the 800 lbs gorilla in the search engine jungle. AltaVista was originally conceived to showcase Digital Equipment Corporation's technology. In the spring of 1995 DEC launched the Alpha 8400, a high performance database server. The AltaVista spider first started indexing the Web on the 4th of July, 1995. A team lead by Dr Louis Monier unveiled AltaVista on the 15th of December 1995. This search engine used several hundred robots running in parallel to index a much larger portion of the Web than predecessors. The system was also fast. Monier's team had growth in mind. The system could be expanded to cope with increasing popularity. More than 300,000 people used the AltaVista on the first day and within 12 months the system was handling 19 million requests per day. For the unsophisticated Web of the mid-1990s it also delivered pretty good results based largely on on-page factors, especially for those searchers who mastered the advanced query interface. AltaVista added more services, in particular Babelfish. Named after a creature in the book The Hitchhiker's Guide to the Galaxy, the Babelfish could automatically translate web pages into a myriad of languages.

AltaBusta

AltaVista's subsequent decline, caused by a mixture of ambition and hubris, should serve as a lesson for anyone who bases their business around the results delivered by a single search engine.

At the start of 1998 Compaq, who'd grown from a maker of luggable IBM PC clones to the world's largest personal computer manufacturer, swallowed the once mighty DEC. It was the 2nd wave of the dot.com boom. Compaq spun out AltaVista with the idea of an Initial Public Offering (IPO). Other search engines such as Yahoo! and Excite had already gone down the same road and had brought their founders and investors vast wealth. However the window of IPO opportunity was fast closing.

By 1999 Search Engines were viewed as being passé. Portals were all the rage. A portal would act as a focus for a surfer's activity on the Web and would provide the owner multiple channels to market products. AltaVista recast itself as a portal and even started to offer Internet access. In the United Kingdom it went as far as to announce unmetered access. This, at a time when AOL, the biggest online provider charged by the hour. Unfortunately for AltaVista the telecommunications market wasn't ready. The botched announcement cost the UK boss, Andy Mitchell his job and damaged AltaVista's reputation.

The move to a portal also detracted from the core search business. Users had to cut through the cruft to get to search then found the results cluttered with sponsored links. It then emerged that, with the notable exception of paid inclusion, the index hadn't been updated in months. By the end of 1999 MSN Search dropped AltaVista as its provider. With stale content and untrustworthy results users began to desert in droves to the simple, search focused interface of new kid: Google. In February 2003 Overture acquired AltaVista for $140 million, a fraction of its $2.3 billion valuation at the height of the dot.com boom. Although they'd survived the dot.bomb this led some wags to dub the search engine: AltaBusta.

AltaVista holds a number of search related US patents including methods for identifying duplicate content in indexes (5,970,497 and 6,138,113) and a method for spidering and indexing the Web (6,021,409)

Anchor Text

Anchor text is highlighted words on a page that link to another web page or resource. Clicking on the text, called hypertext, loads the linked resource in the user's browser. Links are created using the Hypertext Mark-up Language's (HTML) anchor element:

```
<a href="http://www.somedomain.com/new-page.html">This is a
hyperlink</a>
```

The hypertext is the text that occurs between the angle brackets. It would generally appear as: This is a hyperlink in a web browser such as Internet Explorer or Mozilla.

The word hypertext was coined by Ted Nelson who, in the 1960s designed the first ever hypertext system called project Xanadu. Nelson was inspired by a 1945 essay by Vanneva Bush titled: *As We May Think*. In it Bush envisaged a machine where the user could navigate a non-linear path through a trail of documents linked by concepts represented by words or phrases.

Heuristics

While anchor text tells a search engine nothing directly about the contents of the linked page it is used as a convenient heuristic. A heuristic is a rule of thumb that is normally effective in dealing with a given situation but does not absolutely guarantee the desired results. They are shortcuts where a much more detailed and complicated analysis would otherwise be necessary.

In this case the heuristic is to let humans evaluate the content of the target page. The anchor text should then represent in some way the contents of that page. You can think of it as a vote for your page with those keywords. In an ideal world it should be possible to build quite an effective search engine using anchor text alone. Indeed Oliver McBryan who first proposed the idea at the World Wide Web conference in 1994 used this method on his search engine, the WWW Worm.

There are a couple of pitfalls. Firstly many interesting and useful web pages don't have relevant inbound-links. Secondly SEO experts can use this knowledge to subvert a search engine to favor their pages by creating inbound links for popular keyword from other sites under their control. This is a form of search engine spam.

Common Errors

Although the concept of hyper-linking seems natural, many site designers still make basic errors with respect to search engine optimization. For example, say you have created a page about problems with four stroke engines. You may have another page with the following text:

"Problems with modern four stroke engines are rare but do happen."

You could make a link in a number of places:

- <u>Problems</u> with modern four stroke engines are rare but do happen.

- <u>Problems with modern four stroke engines</u> are rare but do happen.

- Problems with modern <u>four stroke engines</u> are rare but do happen.

- Problems with modern four stroke engines are rare but <u>do happen</u>.

You could even link the whole sentence. Although the first and last examples may seem logical the anchor text is too vague to be useful. The page is about four stroke engines, so either option 2 or 3 would be better. There are a number of considerations as to which to use. More keywords in the anchor will dilute the importance the search engine gives to each individual keyword, we may want to rank well for *four stroke* and *four stroke engines* so adding further anchor text could have a negative impact. We would also have to establish how popular each set of keywords is and how much competition there is for each of them. There is no point going head to head with a popular but generic keyword such as *engine* (82 million pages returned by Google) if we are unable to put the resources into getting our page into the first twenty or so results returned by the search engines. This is true no matter how popular the search term. If possible avoid stop words such as *and, by, from, with* as these are not used by search engines when evaluating queries and may dilute the other keywords in the anchor.

How important is Anchor Text?

The top five search engines all put some weight on anchor text. Google currently uses it as a key factor and it is more important than on-page elements. Take the keyword:

```
cycles
```

This returns around 7 million search results in Google. A competitive keyword. The first result is:

```
http://www.raleighbikes.com/
```

If you look at the page source neither the word *cycles* nor the stem word *cycle* are used in the page. The site has a page rank of 6, which is good but not excellent. We can use some special Google options to investigate further. If you search for:

```
allinanchor:cycles
```

Raleigh Bikes is again the top site, this time ranked on in-bound links containing the anchor text with our keyword. Filtering by URL (*allinurl*), title (*allintitle*) and page text (*allintext*) and *Raleigh Bikes* is, as you might already have guessed, nowhere to be found in the first hundred results. This is very interesting and you can find similar results if you dig around a bit. To give you some other well known examples try the keywords: *miserable failure*, which, at the time of writing, brings George Bush's Whitehouse homepage up as number one or *computers*, which shows Apple at number two. Neither keyword is used in the page.

Google Bombing

Miserable failure is part of a phenomenon called Google bombing. A group of individuals create anchor text linking to a certain page on the Web in an effort to bomb it to the top of Google's results pages. Google took a fairly benign attitude to Google bombing until some pranksters linked the phrase "*out-of-touch executives*" to Google's own website. Google was quick to fix this particular example but left some loopholes. For example the phrase "*out of touch management*" combines the highly ranked "*out-of-touch*" anchor text with the word "*management*" found on the page in question:

```
http://www.google.com/corporate/execs.html
```

showing that a mixture of anchor text and good on-page features is still important.

It is amusing to note that neither Yahoo! nor Microsoft's MSN search engine felt it necessary to diffuse this particular Google bomb demonstrating the power of anchor text on those search engines' results pages.

A Word of Caution

Search engine optimizers should exercise some caution. In the examples given it is not necessary for the target page to contain the anchor text. However it would seem reasonable that the anchor pages are at least related to the target in some way. In our example many of the sites linking to Raleigh Bikes were cycle related. If we can spot the relevance it seems likely that Google and other search engines can too, if not today then after the next algorithm update. It would also seem reasonable that anchor text does indeed correspond to the contents of the target page, if only from a user point of view. Remember that these anchors are not there for the benefit of search engines but will direct visitors through to your site.

Anchor Text vs. PageRank

Position	URL	Keyword Density	PR
1	http://www.raleighbikes.com/	0.00	6
2	http://www.sevencycles.com/	0.73	6
3	http://www.evanscycles.com/	1.17	5
4	http://www.intensecycles.com/	13.33	5
5	http://www.yeticycles.com/	5.94	5
6	http://www.salsacycles.com/	1.66	5
7	http://www.bontrager.com/	0.00	5
8	http://www.aardvarkcycles.com/	2.73	5
9	http://www.chainreactioncycles.com/	3.21	5
10	http://www.universalcycles.com/	0.29	5

Table 1. SERPS, PageRank and Anchor Text

Google uses an algorithm called PageRank to assign a value to each page on the Web. There are web based tools that can show this value on a scale of 0 to 10 for a set of results. Checking the PageRank (often abbreviated to PR), for the first 100 sites returned by Google shows that there were a few PR7 sites and at least a dozen other PR6 sites. These included big names of the bike world including the website of Greg Lemond, three times winner of the prestigious Tour de France, now turned cycle manufacturer.

Looking at the top ten, keyword density ranges from 0 to 13.33%. Of course the results will vary over time but unless Google changes its algorithms significantly we can conclude that the separating factor between PR6 sites is relevant anchor text. Anchor text is also more significant than page rank as our top site beats some PR7 sites. Finally Anchor text currently carries more weight than on-page factors such as high keyword density.

Google Search Operators

All the Google Search Operators are fully described on this page:

```
http://www.google.com/help/operators.html
```

Note that *allinanchor* is no longer mentioned on this page and the equivalent: *allinurl* doesn't work.

B

Banning

With Internet search becoming such big business, search engines are keener than ever to ensure the relevance of their results. Search Engine Optimizers have found many clever loopholes in the search algorithms which have enabled them to boost website rankings far beyond what would be justified on content alone.

The search engines have hit back by tweaking and sometimes completely overhauling search algorithms. A good example would be Google's Florida Update in November 2003. Search engines have implemented an array of measures to detect extreme examples of Search Engine Optimization, from discounting those optimizations by lowering the site in the results pages through to outright ban from the index.

Website owners also review their competitors' sites and may report them if they spot any underhand SEO practices. This can result in a review and ban if the site contravenes the engine's terms and conditions. This is probably the most common form of banning. There is a great deal of FUD (Fear, Uncertainty and Doubt) surrounding banning, including the urban legend that a competitor can set up a *spam site* and point links to your pages in order to get them banned. Google has made a statement on this which puts the rumor into perspective:

> *"There is almost nothing a competitor can do to harm your ranking or have your site removed from our index. Your rank and your inclusion are dependent on factors under your control as a webmaster, including content choices and site design."*

There is of course a rub in Google's statement. If your site is then using questionable optimization tactics to boost rankings the fact that someone has linked to your site may draw attention to this fact.

Basically anything that constitutes Black Hat SEO can trigger a ban or penalization. Usually the first a site owner knows about a ban is a rapid fall off in traffic from the search engine in question. This is why it is essential to analyze website traffic and keywords as part of the optimization process. Outright bans are easiest to spot as the traffic from the search engine in question will flat-line. Otherwise you will simply notice a drop in traffic. Remember that a drop in traffic may not be anything sinister and could just be due to other sites targeting the keywords better or to some update to the search engine's algorithms.

Analysis

In the case of a Google ban or penalization, the PageRank reported by their toolbar will often drop to zero for the home page and this will then percolate through to the rest of the site. However the toolbar PR is not particularly accurate and any results should be confirmed by checking rankings in search engines' results pages for target keywords and comparing with previous results.

Figure 1. Zero Page Rank

It should also be remembered that pages take some time, up to several months, to acquire any PageRank and pages deep within a site may never gain enough PageRank to show in the toolbar.

Penalizations are the hardest to spot and are a good reason why any dubious SEO tactics should either be tried on a throwaway test domain or at least restricted to certain pages only. Assuming a global penalization hasn't been imposed it should be possible to identify which optimizations have caused the problem. Check inbound-links to see if any of the sites have been penalized or banned, this may be a clue. If a major link-partner has had its PageRank removed then the value of any inbound-links will also be zero. This will have a knock-on effect on your site. If you have outbound-links to any sites that may be suspect, a link-farm or your SEO Company, check these as well. Your site may have been sucked into a larger ban.

Figure 2. Domain name search results

Sometimes the problem is harder to pin down. A recent poster to an SEO forum wanted to know why his page ranked well with Yahoo! and MSN Search but after a year was still not present in Google for the same keywords. A check showed that he was not in the first 1000 results for his target keywords. However if the test was repeated using the *allinanchor, allinurl, allintext* or *allintitle* operators, the site ranked #1. The site was also in the Google cache and had been visited recently and the Toolbar reported a PageRank of 5, higher than all the competitors. It is possible that some on-page optimizations had triggered the penalty; the keywords were heavily repeated in the title and within the content. The page also did not validate correctly. This shouldn't be a big problem but it arguably makes a search engine robot's job easier if the content is correct HTML. Another problem could have been the multiple inbound-links which originated from a trade directory although these on their own shouldn't cause a problem. The trade directory also ranked well in results pages.

An outright ban is easier to spot. For example when you type in a site's domain name the search engine should rank the site first. In the case of Google it gives the special results page shown in figure 2.

You can also use the Google cache command to see when the page was last visited by Google. As with PageRank if the site or page is new it may not yet have been visited by the robot and so will not be present. What we are talking about is sites that were previously in the search engine's index and have subsequently vanished.

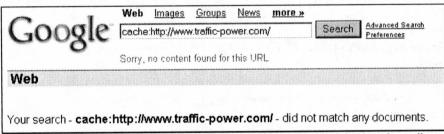

Figure 3. The site's home page is missing from the Google cache, maybe it has been banned?

Finally if a site has been dumped you will either not see it in the search engines results pages or you will get a special screen like this one for MSN Search.

Figure 4. There is no information about the site either

The *site:* operator is also useful to see how many pages the website still has in the search engine index.

```
site:www.traffic-power.com
```

Sometimes the causes of the problems are not obvious. Working with aggressive SEO businesses can lead to a ban for clients. Some unscrupulous SEO operators also use their client's sites to redirect traffic to their own website or to other clients. This may be through hidden links or doorway pages. This can have the knock on effect of getting the client banned even though they were unaware of these tactics.

Relisting

If the penalization or ban has been imposed by some automatic process it is normally a question of identifying the offending optimization, removing it and waiting for the pages to appear again in the results. This can take many months. More serious cases may require human intervention. The process is the same. Aggressive optimizations should be removed from the site and then the search engine firm contacted. Google <help@google.com> seems most responsive to these pleas.

In the worst cases the domain may simply have to be abandoned, the site moved elsewhere and the process of getting re-listed with search-engines, directories and other websites started over.

Reporting SEO Spam

User the following URL to report a site to Google:

```
http://www.google.com/contact/spamreport.html
```

Black Hat SEO

What defines Black Hat SEO (sometimes called *spamdexing*), or even whether the concept really exists at all, is a subject of debate amongst SEO experts. Black-hatters say that ethics do not come into the SEO as any optimizations made to a website are done as a deliberate effort to manipulate search engine results pages. The point of commercial websites, they say, is to make money and to do this they must rank more highly within search engines than their competition. It is up to the search engines to set the parameters of acceptable optimization. The end justifies the means. Others counter that any optimizations that cause a site to rank more highly than its content would otherwise justify or that any changes made specifically for search engines that do not improve the user's experience of the site are Black Hat SEO.

The various search engines set certain guidelines for what they view as acceptable use. These vary and are deliberately vague so as not to give away too much about the algorithms used and to provide a catch-all. For example Yahoo! bans *"pages that provide a poor user experience"*. A very wide ranging and subjective category. However if you step too far over the mark you should not be surprised if your site is penalized or even removed from the index. To further muddy the waters it should be remembered that just as a search engine has no obligation to list your website you have no obligation to abide by the letter of their guidelines. No contract for services has been signed. Most of the websites I have worked on have been indexed through the search engine finding the pages from an inbound-link not through a formal submission process. This supports the attitude that content, layout and structure are the owner's choice and responsibility.

Purely commercial sites, such as online shops, often have little content beyond the products they sell. Adding product reviews, especially where they are generated by users can add useful content. However for most products commercial sites operate in a highly competitive and global marketplace and have to resort to more aggressive SEO techniques in order to rank well. At the extreme end are the *adult content* sites. These frequently use bait-and-switch techniques through doorway pages and have pioneered many other examples of Black Hat optimizations. They operate on quantity, knowing that a small percentage will stay and register even if they were searching for something else.

For many websites high search engine rankings are not the only factor. They want a sticky website, one that the user will explore and come back to later. For a commercial site this will hopefully translate into sales of some kind. This means using search engine optimization that represents the site properly and does not interfere with this secondary goal. For example creating a doorway page that hooks people querying for information on *Basketball* won't please most users if it then leads to information about *Women's Health Issues*.

Examples

Here are some definitions of what Yahoo!, MSN Search and Google consider to be unacceptable SEO (aka spam). This list is not exhaustive. Some of these are discussed in more detail elsewhere.

- Keyword, Anchor Text and Domain Name Stuffing.

- Using hidden text or links. These could be disguised in ALT tags of images or made the same color as the page background so as to appear invisible to the end user. Style Sheets (CSS Spam) can be used in an attempt to hide these manipulations from search engines anti-spam filters.

- Using techniques to artificially increase the number of links to your page, such as link farms or buying and selling links with the main aim of increasing rankings in results pages.

- Excessively cross-linking sites to inflate the apparent popularity.

- Cloaking, delivering different pages depending on the IP address and/or agent who is requesting it.

- Doorway/Gateway/Jump Pages - pages designed as an entrance to a website, each one of them optimized for a different keyword but which have no real content. These automatically redirect the user to the main website. This tactic is heavily used by adult content sites. Often with a JavaScript *mouseover redirect* that sends the user to the new page as soon as the cursor hovers over the page content.

- Duplicate Content. Identical or very similar pages that can be accessed from different URLs. Examples would be copies of the Open Directory Project listings or online books taken from Project Gutenberg. Someone could even steal the content of your website! Google has registered patent number: 6,658,423 aimed at detecting duplicates.

- Auto-generated content of no value to the end user. The aim being to either target keywords or to create excessive internal links.

- Misuse or cyber-squatting of competitor domain names or name typos, for example: Microsofr.com

- Spamming Forums and Weblogs (Blogs).

- Excessive outbound links to websites that use high risk techniques or Spam.

- Hiding outbound-links either with JavaScript or by redirecting to a gateway page blocked by a *robots.txt* file.

- Link Hoarding, getting as many inbound-links while giving out few outbound-links.

Few of these tactics would get a site banned from an index on their own. It is more a pattern of abuse that will trigger penalties. Many of these techniques can be automatically detected by search engine robots when they index the site. Website owners using commercial search engine optimization services should watch out if these tactics are proposed for two reasons. Any business proposing unethical tactics may not be that ethical itself and the optimizations may get the clients banned. There are examples of both happening.

Some Black Hat schemes are more subtle. In the section on PageRank we discuss how the global PageRank available to a site is equivalent to the total number of pages. The structure of a website can be used to distribute this ranking within the site. For example hierarchies feed PageRank back to the top or home page of the site. It would be possible to construct a site where pages below the home page are interconnected and each has a link to the home page. As figure 5 illustrates, a site with only 10 pages and no incoming links the home page has over 3 times the average PageRank of 1.0.

This sort of structure is quite common for presentations and books that should be followed sequentially. Imagine a site with thousands of pages of content. The search engines warn against using automatically generated pages for exactly this reason. However content is freely available on the Web, an example would be the online books available as part of Project Gutenberg. Most of these are now out of copyright and Project Gutenberg puts very limited restrictions on redistribution. It would be feasible to create many pages of content in many different ways and it would be difficult for search engines to automatically classify this as duplicate content. The site structure, while giving a boost to pages at the top of the hierarchy would be in keeping with a book format. Unfortunately there is little new under the sun. If you think up a new SEO angle the chances are it has already been done. In the above example an SEO expert has created just such a classic literature site, it has a healthy PR6 and the owner makes a living from content targeted advertising.

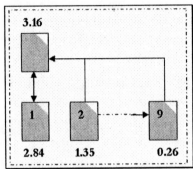

Figure 5. Homepage PageRank increased by site structure

Search Engine Guidelines

Yahoo! Search Site Guidelines:

    http://help.yahoo.com/help/us/ysearch/basics/basics-18.html

Google Information on Search Engine Optimizers:

    http://www.google.com/webmasters/seo.html

MSN Search Guidelines for Webmasters:

    http://search.msn.com/webmasters/guidelines.aspx

Lycos Web Promotion:

    http://webmaster.lycos.co.uk/topics/technic/referencement/refere
    ncement-workshop7/1/

C

Cloaking

Cloaking describes the process of returning different content depending on whether the visitor is a search engine robot or an end user. The content seen by the robot indexing the site can be highly optimized for that search engine and may even be completely different from the page the user will see. Search engines do not like this kind of manipulation of their results and cloaked pages can result in a ban. A software business selling spyware, was kicked off both Google and Yahoo! when, they claim, their SEO company used cloaking to optimize their site. All the more reason to understand the techniques any paid SEO outfit may be thinking of using.

Agent Delivery

Cloaking is performed on the web server. The web page is actually a script. The following code excerpt is written in PHP, a popular web scripting language. It demonstrates the basics of creating a cloaked page. When a browser or spider connects to a web server across the Internet it uses a protocol called the Hyper Text Transfer Protocol or more commonly HTTP. A protocol is a set of rules governing a conversation. As part of the protocol the client sends some information including its address, the type of browser (called the user agent), and the URL of the previous page, if any, that it was visiting.

```
<HTML>
<HEAD><TITLE>Cloaked</TITLE></HEAD>
<BODY>
<?
    $agent = $_SERVER['HTTP_USER_AGENT'];
    if (stristr($agent, "bot")) { ?>
        Search Engine Optimized
<? } else {?>
        User Friendly
<? } ?>
</BODY>
```

If the User Agent contains the string *bot* (as in Googlebot, MSNbot etc.) then we can assume the client is a robot indexing our site and we can serve a search engine friendly page, otherwise we serve an end-user version of the page. Our search engine friendly version could contain a number of spam techniques such as keyword stuffing.

This is quite a simplistic example and is fairly easy to detect. For example the version of the page held in the Yahoo! or Google cache would differ from that served to the end user. Someone could also connect to the site using the cUrl (command line URL) utility.

```
curl --user-agent "Googlebot/2.1
(+http://www.googlebot.com/bot.html)"
http://www.cloakedsite.com/
```

This would return the cloaked version of the page. A more sophisticated cloaking scheme would also check the client IP address. For example, recently the Googlebot has been using IP addresses in the range 64.68.80.01 to 64.68.87.254. After determining the User Agent the cloaked page could then see if the client address falls within this range. Robots also normally have a blank Referrer field.

This requires that the cloaker maintains an accurate and up-to-date list of the addresses used by robots and also has a list of exceptions. We wouldn't want to serve a cloaked page to the Google language translation service. We should also keep our cloaked page from being cached by including the

```
<META HTTP-EQUIV="CACHE-CONTROL" CONTENT="NO-CACHE">
```

or

```
<META NAME="robots" CONTENT="noarchive">
```

meta tags in the Head section of the cloaked version of the web page. This may be a clue in itself that the page is cloaked.

IP Address Delivery

Commercial cloaking software is available to manage cloaked pages. Normally this will include automatic updates for the list of addresses used by search engine spiders and their user agent names as well as addresses that should be excluded. This can make the detection of cloaked pages difficult but not completely impossible.

There are some good reasons for serving different pages based on the User Agent and other HTTP fields. SEOers originally used it to stop people stealing the optimized versions of their pages. Another reason is that formatting often differs between browser types and versions. This process could be used to serve different style sheets depending on whether the browser was Internet Explorer or Mozilla. A website may wish to exclude certain countries based on domain or IP address. Finally it is useful for serving up web pages localized for different languages by using the HTTP_ACCEPT_LANGUAGE variable.

Competition

It is important to remember that you are not just trying to second guess how search engines work but are competing with thousands of other websites to get into the top ten of search engine results pages. In the SEO game there are only a few winners for a given set of keywords. Beating the competition is not a question of luck or chance but strategy. A campaign should be planned by selecting keywords, then studying the competition, analyzing their tactics and then either doing it better or targeting points of weakness.

Analysis Techniques

Typing your target keywords into a search engine only tells you the total number of results for those keywords not how hard it will be to get a top ten site ranking. Many of the pages are not even trying to compete for the keyword and are there by chance. To find the real competition you need to dig a little deeper. The first thing anyone might do to optimize their page is to include the keywords in the title. Google provides some useful advanced search operators that can help in this analysis. Entering

```
intitle:kw1 kw2... kw#
```

Will return all the pages where the keywords occur somewhere in the title. Putting the keywords in quotes means that the exact phrase must occur in the title, an even stronger indicator that they are your direct competition. You can also use *allintitle* which will match against the keywords in the order given. For example the keywords: laptop computer parts, returns 4.1 million results. In terms purely of PageRank you'd need to be a PR6 or PR7 site to compete in this space, quite a tall order. However the search:

```
intitle:laptop computer parts
```

returns 321,000 results. That is only around 8% of sites are competing for those keywords. Searching for the exact phrase:

```
intitle:"laptop computer parts"
```

returns only 779 pages.

The clincher will be off-page factors. We want to find out how many of those pages also have the keywords in the anchor text (hypertext links) of either internal or inbound-links. We can do this with the search:

```
intitle: "kw1 kw2... kw#" inanchor: "kw1 kw2... kw#"
```

In our example we are left with a hardcore of 114 websites. The top ten had toolbar PageRanks between PR0 and PR5. We can use the Google *link* operator to see how many inbound-links each page in the top ten has. However Google doesn't show a lot of inbound-links below PR4. Yahoo! appears to report much more accurate figures. The query:

Will give the number of inbound-links excluding internal-links. Remember that internal links do count and you have complete control over the anchor text. We don't know how many of these inbound-links use relevant anchor text. This would require a more detailed analysis of the results pages. The result set can be further divided by using the *inurl* and *intext* operators to find pages with the keywords in the URL and in the body text of the page. Running this query left a total of 58 results, barely 0.00014% of the original figure.

We could also check the keyword density of the competitor pages and the total number of pages on their site. The query *site:www.domain.com* gives the total number of pages indexed by Google or Yahoo! As a general rule more pages in a website means better rankings. As an example the top ranked site on Google is currently Microsoft.com (search for the keyword *http* in Google to see the top ranked websites) with 314,000 pages indexed covering a vast range of computer related keywords.

SEO is an ongoing process. Other sites will be fine tuning their on and off page optimizations in order to maintain or improve their ranking. The Google operators we have looked at can be used to prioritize the areas that need attention on existing pages. We'll assume that the page URL and Title already contain the relevant keywords. Here are some examples:

- **inanchor position higher than search engine ranking:** focus attention on on-page factors: title tags, content, keyword density, headings, bold/strong text, site structure.

- **inanchor position lower than search engine ranking:** build inbound links with relevant keywords in anchor text.

- **good ranking but smaller site compared to competition:** add new content focusing on target keyword combinations.

Content Management Systems (CMS)

Content Management Systems (CMS) are becoming increasingly popular for managing today's large and complex websites. The actual content of the website is held in a database; MySql is a very popular relational database choice as it is free and is often supplied as part of a web hosting package. The content is retrieved from the database and packaged into web pages by a software system running on the web server. The format of the pages can be highly customized by using templates and style sheets (CSS). From the user viewpoint the site looks like normal web pages.

Content Management Systems let website owners concentrate on the information in the site without worrying about detail such as creating pages in the Hyper Text Markup Language (HTML). Many large websites, particularly anything interactive such as news sites, blogs and forums are driven by CMS. Complex sites that have specific requirements will write their own software but many off-the-shelf packages, both free and commercial, are available. These are often written in the PHP or Perl programming languages. As with MySQL these two computer languages are free and frequently come as an integral part of web hosting packages. Search engines can spider Perl, PHP, ASP.Net, Coldfusion, Python and Java amongst other languages providing the pages are reachable. *Moveable Type* and *pMachine* are amongst the most popular Content Management Systems.

Just as the standard look and feel of a CMS will not suit most websites they are also poorly optimized for search engines straight out of the box. The focus of CMS designers is information delivery to human users not search engine robots. There are a number of customizations that make Content Management Systems more search engine friendly.

Dynamic URLs

A Content Management Systems is usually implemented as a collection of scripts. These retrieve data based on some parameters passed as part of the Uniform Resource Locator (URL). As an example the following link could be on the homepage of a website. It calls the *content* script located in the home directory of the website: *www.mydomain.com*

```
http://www.mydomain.com/content.php?story=137&lang=en
```

Judging by the file extension, the script is written in the PHP programming language. The script is passed two parameters: *story* and *lang*. These are set to *137* and *en* respectively. The script would probably go to a database and retrieve the content using these two parameters as a key. Finally the program wraps the content in HTML and returns it to the user.

This type of URL is called dynamic and these are probably the first thing to tackle as some search engines find them hard to read, especially where a number of parameters are used. Google will index (spider) dynamic URLs but claims that it will do this more slowly as generating dynamic content puts a load on the web server. The new MSN search will only spider up to an absolute maximum of 5 query terms. They are worried about spider traps. This is where the search engine robot gets stuck crawling through every permutation of the query parameters.

The first point to check is whether the CMS serves consistent and spiderable URLs. If the website cannot be accessed by a machine beyond the homepage, or the URLs change with each access the content will not get indexed. A clue to problems is analyzing the log files, see if search engine robots are visiting the home page but explore no further.

It is a good idea to turn dynamic URLs into pseudo static versions. This is discussed in a little more detail in the database driven content section. It consists of replacing the separators in the query string with forward slashes:

```
http://www.mydomain.com/content/137/en
```

and then using some jiggery-pokery on the web server to make sure that the content-management-system program still gets called when the URL is accessed. This technique is called URL rewriting.

Outbound-Links

Many content management systems generate too many links on each page of the site. They seem to do this because it is easy for the CMS developer. These links rarely use relevant anchor text and can distribute PageRank and visitors in undesirable ways.

Start by removing links to moderators, user profiles and member lists. There are malicious robots out there that can search member lists to extract email addresses to use for sending spam emails. Each outbound-link is a possibility for the user to exit the page, so focus the user and search engine robots on the site's content and not extraneous information. If these links are useful make them available only to authenticated users, that way they are hidden from search engine robots.

Icons

Icons (small graphics) such as next or previous story buttons should either be replaced with text links or relevant ALT (alternative) text should be used in the image.

Sessions and Authentication

Make sure that search engine robots can access the site content without having to log-in. For example many forums are configured to only permit authenticated users to view the site contents. Session ids are used as part of authentication or standalone to track users across the site. These are implemented either using cookies or by adding an id to the URL. Robots can't manage cookies and any session ids added to the web address present problems similar to dynamic URLs. They will almost certainly no longer be valid by the time the robot visits other pages on the site.

Extraneous Content

Any text not directly relevant to the content should be removed. This includes statistics, member signatures, profiles, repetitive text and images. These dilute the content especially for non-authenticated users. On blogs and forums link member names to their posts, this acts like a mini sitemap directing robots to deep or old content. Similarly create a page with most commented or viewed articles; these should use relevant anchor text.

Make sure that generated content uses correct Title and Header elements. The title and headers should contain the page's target keywords. Each content page can link back to the site's home with the main target keywords. This can be done through a text link or an image with relevant ALT text.

All pages should be optimized for load speed and should not be greater than 100K and probably closer to 10K in length. Some search engines will not index more than the first few paragraphs of a page and even Google says that its robots will give up on slow or very long pages.

Forums

Websites with lots of fresh content are favored by search engines. Large websites cover many keywords and also have a lot of internal links with the potential for generating PageRank and anchor text. Creating content takes effort so some SEO experts suggest running a forum as an adjunct or even as the main website. A forum is just another form of CMS. *phpBB* is one of the more popular forum packages. It requires web hosting with MySQL and PHP installed.

The beauty of a forum is that the users generate the content; all the website owner has to do is install and administer the software. The first problem is gaining enough users to make the forum a worthwhile place to visit. This will require some good marketing and a lack of established competitors. Forums are generally fairly small communities frequently with a cabal of regular posters even if they have a lot of lurkers (people who read but don't contribute). Where the posters do contribute interesting content this is not a problem but sometimes the discussions generate into slanging matches called flame-wars. These can even turn libelous which may cause legal problems for the forum owner. Forums can also use a great deal of bandwidth. Most hosting packages charge for bandwidth and a high traffic forum can cost hundreds of dollars in hosting fees.

The best forums generate a lot of inbound-links, either to the forum home or to interesting threads. Optimization is the same as with other CMS with a few specifics. Each post should link back to the home page of the site. The *Previous* and *Next* links on each post should be hidden from search engines, either through user agent delivery techniques or by masking from non-authenticated users. On many Content Management Systems these links change depending on the most recent replies to topics. This is very confusing to search engine robots.

Do not underestimate how much time it will take to administer a forum and this may detract from running the main business. Where a forum has responsible users some of them can be appointed moderators. The moderators will need to watch out for content copied directly from other sites which may cause copyright issues, for libelous postings and for spammers including links to their own sites in the hope of boosting rankings.

It seems that as far as Google is concerned forums don't have too much effect as a source of inbound-links. Google either has some way of identifying forum generated content or the dynamic nature of most forums means that content moves off the home and main index pages before it gets indexed.

Site Maps

Where it is difficult to make the dynamic content spiderable a sitemap can be used. This would be a collection of static links, with relevant anchor text, pointing to the dynamic content. Of course, as a sitemap is static it rather negates some of the advantages of dynamic content and will have to be regenerated on a regular basis. Large amounts of content will also create large sitemaps which may take a long time to get fully indexed.

Security Holes

Running any kind of CGI program, including custom or off-the-shelf Content Management Systems, increases the risk that a website will be compromised by hackers. The risks include: defacement of the content, use of the website to send spam emails, storing pirated software and information theft. Shopping sites pose the greatest threats as a break-in may leave customer data, including credit-card information vulnerable. Web security is beyond the scope of this book but the following are some basic security measures to obscure useful information from hackers.

Many Content Management Systems include a link back to the software author. This is nice for them as it is a source of inbound-links, frequently from highly ranked home pages. This is why a site such as phpBB currently has a Google PageRank of 9. However it gives potential hacker information about your CMS system. Say you are running *pMachine version 2.3*. A hacker can search for security bulletins on Bugtraq or SecurityFocus relating to this system. Even easier is to start with a list of bugs then search Google for the string "powered by *<cms name>*" to find sites using that system.

It is therefore a good idea to hide any information about the CMS in both the content and the URLs:

```
http://www.aforum.com/phpBB/index.php
```

Dynamic URLs should be rewritten to be static in any case.

Similarly the paths to administration or form processing scripts should be changed. Many malicious robots roam the web searching for loopholes in website installations. In the last month one of my sites has had the following pages probed by automatic tools

- /scripts/formmail.pl
- /cgi-bin/formdecode.cgi
- /cgi-bin/request.cgi
- /brownsenquiry.cgi
- /cgi-bin/formmail/formmail.cgi
- /cgi-bin/form.cgi
- /cgi-bin/recommend.pl
- /cgi-bin/BFormMail.pl
- /cgi-bin/mailform.pl

These are standard locations for mail processing scripts included with many CMS packages. A spammer could use these to send out unsolicited commercial email, scams and viruses. *Spambots*, automated scripts to post comment spam, are also frequent visitors

Content Targeted Advertising

In the heady days of the dot.com boom webmasters could generate a reasonable revenue stream from banner adverts. These are images placed along the top of web pages. CPM rates (cost per 1000 views) of $50 were not unheard of. Banner adverts frequently advertised other websites and were paid for with money from venture capital or the IPO. With the collapse of the dot.coms advertising dried to a trickle and rates plummeted.

Many surfers developed a condition dubbed *banner blindness*. The more in-the-face banners became the more users were able to mentally screen them out. Response or click-through rates were abysmal. With a return to reality many advertisers preferred to develop partnerships with websites using affiliate services such as Commission Junction and paying commissions on leads or sales.

In a search for a revenue stream some search engines started offering sponsored links. These links were related to the search query and where they were clearly differentiated from the results they could be valuable to both searcher and advertiser alike. Pricing was still problematic. eBay had shown the way with online auctions and Overture obtained a patent for the process of running a keyword auction. In this advertisers bid for search queries and the highest bids have their links placed next to the results pages.

AdWords and AdSense

In 2000 Google launched its AdWords system based on a similar idea. Google added the twist of ranking advertisements according to their popularity. If more people click on an advertisement further down the list it will be moved up even if other advertisers are bidding more for the query.

In the autumn of 2003 Google extended this system to third party websites calling the new program AdSense. Webmasters could include some JavaScript code on their page and Google in turn would display adverts relevant to the content of the page. AdSense does this by indexing a page using its own robot called *Mediabot*. The User Agent string is:

```
Mediapartners-Google/2.1
```

When a user visits an AdSense enabled page that has not yet been indexed the AdSense code causes the page to be added to a queue. Mediabot then visits shortly afterwards. Using a separate robot ensures *Chinese walls* are maintained between search and advertising and that the robot is tailored towards the needs of Content Targeted Advertising (CTA). The key to AdSense adverts are that they are unobtrusive and relevant to the content. Google uses technology called CIRCA acquired from Applied Semantics to help them understand the content of pages although adverts can be based on a single element, say the page title. Click through rates are monitored to control the quality of the adverts served.

The AdSense system gives webmasters a great deal of control over the look and feel of their adverts. A web based control panel offers a set of layout formats: banner, skyscraper etc. with some predefined color schemes. The latter can be customized further by skilled webmasters to fit in with the design of the site. For each advert that a user clicks a percentage of the fee is passed to the website. Earnings vary for different keywords or even from day to day depending on what advertisers are bidding. Google does not allow members of the AdSense program to discuss their earnings but each click earns in the region of 20 to 40 cents with click through rates ranging from 2.5% to over 4%. Higher value products or services can bid a great deal more for keywords. This is where some very specialized and targeted pages, for instance: *loans*, or *asbestosis*, can earn good money with only a trickle of visitors.

Using the lower figure from above, a site with a million page views per month would earn $60,000 per year. Unlike the Overture advertising program Google will accept sites with low monthly page views; the only proviso is that a payout is made once earnings reach $100. AdSense generated a lot of excitement when it was launched in 2003 and has enabled many webmasters to at least cover expenses. More expert SEOers have been able to earn a living from AdSense alone.

AdSense Optimization

AdSense and similar programs have had an impact on search engine optimization and the design of websites. To increase content targeted advertising revenues websites have a number of options:

1. increase the number of page views

2. increase the click through rate

3. target higher value keywords

The number of page views can be increased by increasing the number of visitors to a site. A site that has undergone no serious optimization should be able to significantly increase its AdSense revenues by applying just some of what is described in this book. Page views can also be increased by adding more content and by splitting larger pages. This last point has an impact on site ranking. Smaller pages can be more focused and can target high value keyword niches. This means that more effective search engine optimization tactics can be applied and that the adverts should be more relevant to the content. Ideally each page should be about a screen of text covering a single subject. That way adverts will remain on the screen while the content is read.

Webmasters should also experiment with different ad formats, color schemes and page positioning. Google permits multiple AdSense blocks on a page. So a single image banner advert could be mixed with text adverts on the right margin of the page or adverts could be placed directly within the content at various points.

Advertisers can create or optimize pages for higher value keywords. Obviously some analysis will need to be made against how often searchers query for those keywords. An AdWords account will show what is being bid for those keywords.

AdSense adverts are separate from Google search. That means that surfers arriving from Yahoo! MSN Search and other channels will also see the adverts so it can be worthwhile to put some effort into optimizing the pages for those search engines.

There are problems. Some advertisers have noticed a drop off in click-through rates (CTR) over time. This may be related to the number of advertisers bidding for keywords relevant to the site. A small advertiser pool will mean that the same adverts will be recycled. If the site has a high number of repeat visitors they will quickly develop *AdSense blindness*. Sudden traffic surges, perhaps due to some article capturing the interest of a wider audience, do not seem to transfer to higher revenues. Maybe these visitors are more focused on the web page content than a random cross-section of visitors. AdSense also requires visitors to have JavaScript enabled on their browsers. Some firms do not allow this on their employees' desktops for security reasons. Google is sometimes unable to serve relevant adverts for a page. This is the case for new pages not yet visited by Mediabot. Mediabot also seems to be amnesiac and forgets about pages that it has not visited for a while. Google serves so called *public service* adverts when it is unable to find anything relevant. These do not earn money for the site and will only be related to the site's content by chance. Google permits the website to serve alternative adverts in this case. These can be from an affiliate scheme or from another CTA program.

Scams and Click Fraud

Now readers may be wondering what prevents them from signing up for an advertising program and clicking on the adverts themselves. In theory, nothing at all and this idea hasn't escaped a number of scammers. Stories abound of armies of Indians and Chinese sitting in cyber cafés busily clicking on adverts and paid a commission by unscrupulous webmasters. CTA programs monitor clicks. A series of accesses from the same computer over a short time frame to diverse ad programs would be sure to arouse suspicion. Some programs bar access to users in China or India or those accessing the Web from certain anonymous proxy servers. Websites attracting unusually high click through rates or other activity may be investigated and barred. Sites that have been booted out of Google's AdSense program have complained bitterly about what they see as the arbitrary nature of such bans with little chance of appeal. Still the problem of fraudulent clicks is serious for advertisers. One user of Overture estimates that around 20% of their clicks are fraudulent - that is clicks from the same IP address or suspicious visitors that don't go beyond the entry page. Most programs allow advertisers to block specific addresses but this is only a partial solution.

In a recent interview with CNN Money, Google's Chief Financial Officer George Reyes claimed that click-fraud was the most urgent issue facing the search engine company as it potentially threatens their business model. Reyes said that perpetrators appear to be the competitors of advertisers and also scam sites set up for the sole purpose of hosting ad links provided by Google and other CTA firms. Google will be launching an AdSense API which will give advertisers more control over the AdSense program.

Apart from fraud detection Google is taking direct measures. Last month it filed a civil lawsuit against a Texas-based Internet company, Auctions Expert International that signed up for the AdSense program in 2003. Google claims that the company defrauded Google and its advertisers by systematically clicking on ads for its own financial benefit.

ClickBots

Michael Anthony Bradley a 32 year old American hacker who went by the handle of CountScoobula touted a program called *Google Clique*. He claimed that this could generate revenue of around $30,000 per month by automatically clicking on AdSense links. Bradley offered his program to the world after a fruitless attempt to sell his knowledge directly to Google. He described a meeting with Google engineers in March 2004. The Google guys were apparently very friendly, they asked him lots of questions but Bradley was surprised that they seemed to have little programming knowledge. During the meeting he is said to have joked that his approach looked like *"blackmail"*.

A week later Bradley was arrested and charged by Federal Agents for attempting to extort $100,000 from Google. Bradley had a lot of knowledge about AdSense. His program kept the overall click-through rate at around 1.2% and used complex tunneling technology to randomize IP addresses.

Other scamsters have used ClickBots to try to get competitor websites pulled from CTA programs or to manipulate the auctions that decide pricing. The ClickBot passes its requests through anonymous Internet proxies, changing client information and running the AdSense JavaScript code to select links at random. They target quiet periods so that the increase in clicks doesn't trigger any alarms. A ClickBot or proxy could also be installed on random machines on the Internet using a worm or virus making detection almost impossible.

Other CTA Programs

Although webmasters are currently reporting good results with Google AdSense there are alternative content targeted advertising networks, some are listed in the search engine FAQ:

```
http://www.internet-search-engines-faq.com/google-adsense-
alternatives.shtml
```

AdSense Sandbox

The sandbox claims to show the Google AdSense links that will be displayed on a particular web page:

```
http://www.digitalpoint.com/tools/adsense-sandbox/
```

D

Database Driven Content

Many organizations have information held in a database which they would like to make available over the Web. This data also represents potential content that can be indexed by search engines. More content means more keyword coverage, more PageRank to be distributed within the site and more potential relevant anchor text in links.

The database will usually be accessible through an HTML form interface. This allows the user to retrieve data based on some search parameters. Forms are too complicated for search engine robots to use so an alternative approach is needed. The data can either be exported to a set of static pages or it can be accessed programmatically in a search engine friendly way.

It seems a pity to turn all that nice, dynamic data into a set of static pages. If the database is rarely or never updated this can be a satisfactory approach at the risk of duplicating the amount of data to be stored. The programmatic approach has the advantage of centralizing the data in one place at the expense of performance and complexity. Each time a page is accessed a program is run on the web server which then retrieves the data from the database management system (DBMS). What is effectively being created is a bespoke Content Management System with all that implies in terms of project management, cost and security implications.

As an example we may have a database that holds information on motorcars. I worked on just such as system as part of the *OneSwoop.com* online car retailer. The data is organized as manufacturer, model name and description. To make the URLs search engines friendly we could structure the system so that the resource:

```
http://www.mysite.com/cars
```

retrieves information about all the car manufacturers in the database, it is effectively a content page and an entry point to the cars database. The page is a Common Gateway Interface program (CGI) that selects all of the car manufacturers from the database and displays them as a series of hyperlinks.

Clicking on the link:

```
cars/ford
```

will retrieve all the car models that Ford manufacturers from the database, displaying each one as a hyperlink. Finally:

```
cars/ford/focus
```

retrieves information about the Ford Focus from the database. From a search engine viewpoint it is accessing a hierarchy of static pages. From a programmer's viewpoint there may be a single program that uses information in the URL to decide what action to perform. Now if you are familiar with web programming you may remember that parameters to a program are normally passed in a section of the URL called the query string, that is, everything after the question mark '?':

```
cars?manufacturer=ford&model=focus
```

Here the *cars* CGI script is passed the manufacturer and model name as parameters. A search engine may index only the root *cars* page and some dislike following links with query strings. They are said to be search engine unfriendly. The solution is to create pseudo static URLs that look like the ones we saw earlier in this section and then use some trickery to extract the parameters. The popular Apache server has an extension called *mod_rewrite* that can do this for us. Users of Microsoft's Internet Information Server (IIS) should check out *ISAPI Rewrite*. Both are powerful but have a complicated syntax.

Directories

Directories started life as an eclectic list of a web surfer's favorite sites, for example *Jerry and David's guide to the World Wide Web*, which was the original name of the Yahoo! Directory. Directories are important for optimizers because they provide inbound-links from popular sites and can help a page get indexed rapidly by search engines. They are also a source of annoyance for webmasters. In the early days the people building directories were only too happy to get suggestions of interesting new websites. However as the Web grew many directories became inundated with requests and either started taking inordinate amounts of time to include sites or began charging for inclusion.

Submission

Many webmasters get frustrated with directories because they don't read the submission guidelines first. These vary from directory to directory but in general to get listed a site must offer something to the visitors of the directory. This means original content. Affiliate sites that are just a restyled front-end to another website will only get listed if they provide something extra, such as product reviews. Sites should have a reasonable number of pages, these should be written in correct HTML with no broken links and viewable on a range of browsers, operating systems and screen resolutions. Remember that the editor who checks your site may use Mozilla on Linux or Safari on an Apple Mac. Sites should be finished; an *under construction* logo is a sure way to get rejected. The web server that hosts the site should also be reliable, long periods of downtime will mean that the editor cannot check the site and may result in existing directory entries being dropped. Check the appropriate categories by looking at the current entries. Some directories will only allow first submissions at the bottom of the directory tree. Prepare your site information; you will need the title, a short description and long description. This should be factual and not contain hype; phrases like *"the best resource"* or *"the number one"* are subjective and will almost certainly be rejected.

DMOZ and Yahoo! Directory

The two principal directories are DMOZ (aka the Open Directory Project: <http://dmoz.org/>) and Yahoo Directory! <http://dir.yahoo.com/>. Both offer free inclusion and both can take an age to include new websites. DMOZ provides listings for the Google directory and, because it is open, is probably one of the most widely copied directories on the Web. A single entry can easily provide dozens of inbound-links from various sites although Google's duplicate page algorithms will eliminate many of these from the index.

To suggest a site, browse to the appropriate category and click on the *suggest link* text. It is worth submitting to both Google and Yahoo! as they can boost ranking in respective search engines. The inclusion process can be expedited in Yahoo! by paying a fee.

Zeal

Zeal is also popular and supplies results to the LookSmart directory. Users must register and pass an online exam to submit a site. Submissions must then be approved by an editor. Read the guidelines very carefully as rejections are common. Other web directories can be found by querying search engines.

Although directories do not provide a huge amount of traffic as most people use search engines they are an additional source of visitors which can help protect against major updates in search engine algorithms. Not all directory listings are worthwhile. Watch out for zero PageRank pages, maybe they are not indexed by Google and other search engines. PageRank dilution is also a problem, the outbound-links on a directory's nice PR6 page may be spread over hundreds of sites. Be careful about directories that require you to link back to them but then try to stop any PageRank leakage by redirecting your site through another page or use JavaScript link cloaking.

Keep a record of the directories and categories you submit to and periodically check to see if your site has been included. This also stops you resubmitting to the same directory.

Paid Submissions

Paid directory submissions should be treated like any other paid inbound-link, they will generate a small amount of traffic but their worth is largely in terms of anchor text and PageRank. For example the Microsoft Small Business directory currently charges $49 for submission. If you look at the directory with the Google toolbar installed they are at best selling a PR6 page with around 30 outbound links and at worst a PR0 page. Is that worth making a very rich man even richer?

Other Directories

DMOZ has a listing of over 1000 web directories including many niche and country specific sites:

```
http://dmoz.org/Computers/Internet/Searching/Directories/
```

and the Search Engine FAQ has a useful table that includes regional directories and a list of the ones that have included the author's site

```
http://www.internet-search-engines-faq.com/submit-url-free-
directory.shtml
```

Domain Cloaking

Many individuals and small companies have web space as part of their Internet connection. However they don't want to run a site called something like: *mydomain.some-isp.com*, because it doesn't look professional and it causes problems if the person moves their Internet Service Provider (ISP). A cheap and cheerful solution is to buy a domain from a domain registry. When a user connects to the website: *www.mydomain.com*, the domain registry sends a special message to the browser called a Moved Temporarily redirect containing the address of the real web server. The browser will then connect to this address.

The Uniform Resource Locator in the browser's address toolbar will be that of the ISP hosted website, not the domain hosted by the registry. This has a number of disadvantages. Search engines will see two domains, anyone linking to the site will be confused as to which domain to use and for businesses it looks unprofessional. Most domain registries offer a solution called Domain Cloaking, Masked or Stealth Redirection. The term Domain Cloaking sometimes leads to confusion with Page Cloaking.

Problems with Framesets

Domain Cloaking uses HTML Framesets. These split a page into separate panes that obtain their contents from other web pages. These pages can be on the local or remote server. The framed page itself is hosted by the domain registry and it is normally possible to specify the page title and some keywords and a description.

```
<frameset rows="100%,*" border="0" frameborder="0">
 <frame name="__main" src="http://www.mydomain.com/" noresize
frameborder="0">
</frameset>
```

The problem is that the amount of content that can be included in the Frameset is a long way from what we would require for engine optimization. Worse still, it is generic for the whole site. Some search engines won't understand the Frame element and won't index the real site content. Other search engines that do understand Frames will index the content, but at its real address. In addition users will not be able to bookmark pages and will have trouble deep linking to your website as the URL shown in the browser address bar will always be the homepage.

Anyone serious about Search Engine Optimization will get proper web hosting. By all means forward other domains to this account but avoid this type of stealthy redirection.

Duplicate Content

A great deal of the Web is duplicate or near-duplicate content. Documents may be served in different formats: HTML, PDF, Text for different audiences. Documents may get mirrored to avoid delays or to provide fault tolerance. Content is syndicated and re-branded for different audiences and markets. Some websites aggregate or incorporate content from other sources on the Web. Press releases are often duplicated by many media outlets. Businesses wishing to protect their trademarks frequently register different versions of their name which all point to the same content but look like different websites from the point of view of a search engine.

Finally there is a problem of plagiarism and copying from public domain sources, such as Wikipedia, the Open Directory Project and Project Gutenberg. This is often done to create large, content rich sites to manipulate search engine rankings and generate revenue based on Content Targeted Advertising.

When users submit queries to search engines they do not want the results pages stuffed with many duplicate or near duplicate pages. Indexing and filtering near duplicate content also puts a load on search engines in terms of storage and computational resources. Algorithms already exist for efficiently classifying duplicate content. For example a Hash function can generate a numeric fingerprint representing a page's content. Pages with identical fingerprints can be dropped from search results and excluded by robots when they next index pages.

Near duplicate pages are more complicated. Both AltaVista (now owned by Yahoo! - patents: 5,970,497 and 6,138,113) and Google have been awarded US patents (6,615,209 and 6,658,423) that improve on existing methods for classifying duplicate content. The secret is to make comparisons quickly without doing some kind of word-by-word matching. One of AltaVista's patents looks for similarities in the outbound links on a page. Google's patents focus on generating hashes or fingerprints for parts rather than the whole page. Now to you and me neither of these ideas would seem to be that novel and probably took less than a wet Sunday afternoon in Menlo Park to conceive but you have to remember that the US patent office also gave a patent for how to use a garden swing (US Patent No. 6,368,227). The patent land-grab is more to have some bargaining chips with other companies; many would stand up about as well as a beach condo in a Florida hurricane if tested in court. However they do have the effect of discouraging new entrants to the market.

Google's patents are capable of identifying duplicate content that is a subset of another document. The inventors suggest that the most relevant document is returned in the results pages. This could be the most recent (although to my mind most recent would imply a copy) or the document with the highest PageRank. Probably the biggest target in Google's sights at the moment is the many duplicates of public domain content such as Wikipedia. Some webmasters have found their original pages have been dropped in favor of mirrors so the system is not without flaws. The system should also foil domain spammers who register many different domain names under different keywords all pointing to the same website.

E

Entry and Exit Pages

Entry pages are any page that brings traffic to your website. They are usually well optimized for popular keywords and have inbound-links which may have been posted on blogs or forums. An entry page can be anywhere on your website.

While many sites are focused around the homepage, as a site adds content it begins to build sections of themed content centered on hubs. These hubs are effectively home pages in their own right. They concentrate internal links and should target the most popular and competitive keywords appropriate to the theme. It should be possible to navigate to the rest of the site from the entry page, in particular to pages within the theme and to the home page where other hubs should be reachable. The site branding should be obvious. The term Entry Page is also used to describe doorway or jump pages.

An exit page is the last page a user visits before leaving the site. You can't expect a user to stay on one website forever so it is normal that they will head off at some point, either through an outbound-link or by going to a site they've bookmarked or entered directly into the address bar. There may be some reason why a user exits the site at a certain point; maybe the page does not link to other interesting content. The route a user takes from the entry to exit page is called a *path*.

Everflux

Traditionally Google makes one major update per month. This is dubbed the Googledance as rankings in the results pages change erratically, particularly between the various data centers that serve Google's results.

This is then followed by visits from the Googlebots, the results of which are fed into the next dance. Since around mid-2002 webmasters noticed that sites were being spidered on a more continuous basis. This crawl is an attempt to identify new or updated content in order to keep the Google index fresh. It is neither as broad nor as deep as the regular indexing process. It can also produce some strange effects where new sites are located by an inbound-link or submission to Google. Some content gets indexed and shows up in the results pages only to be dropped, sometimes for a couple of months before the main crawl indexes the site.

When a user goes to *www.google.com* they are in fact being routed to one of thousands of computers that process queries. The routing is handled by load-balancing, either by the Internet naming system (DNS) returning different addresses for the domain or by front-end techniques entirely transparent to the end user. Google's computers are built out of cheap, off-the-shelf components running the Linux operating system and are mainly located in data centers in California and Virginia. Google is thought to have a number of separate copies of its index located across these computers. The same search can yield slightly different results depending on which copy of the index is used.

The effect of continuously fluctuating search results has been dubbed Everflux by search engine experts.

Florida Update

Early in November 2003 Google watchers started to notice some odd behavior with their favorite search engine. The Google Toolbar frequently showed the PageRank for sites as grayed out and this was coupled with big changes in the results for keywords they were tracking. Watchers also witnessed discrepancies between the various data centers, a sure indication that a major re-indexing of the database, called a Googledance, was underway.

By the 14th of November it was clear that Google had made a serious update to their algorithms with many commercial and highly optimized sites heavily penalized in the search rankings especially on two and three keyword searches. In the all important pre-Christmas shopping period the change couldn't have come at a worse time. This update has been dubbed Florida, following the nomenclature used by hurricane forecasters. It certainly looked like a lot of websites were reaping a whirlwind. SEO pundits immediately started scrambling for theories as to what had happened and how the effects could be mitigated.

What Happened?

Immediately after the update some people noticed that putting one or two nonsense terms after the query terms caused Google to deliver very different search results. For example a search for: *digital cameras* returns about 8 million results but *digital cameras dkjfdlajd* returns nothing because our nonsense word *dkjfdlajd* can't be found in any page. If we search for the original term but now specifically exclude our nonsense word:

```
digital cameras -dkjfdlajd
```

we would expect that excluding a word that does not occur anywhere in the Google index would have no effect on results but in fact they appeared similar to those given before the Florida update. This glitch was patched by Google in early December although the Scroogle site <www.scroogle.org> has a page that claims it can show pre-Florida search results using another loophole.

Money Words

Theories abound for what was causing these strange results. One idea, related to the fact that commercial sites had been most affected, was that Google was pre-filtering searches for so called *money words* using a poisoned word list. Speculation was that these words were compiled by analyzing popular phrases from its AdWords system. This would then force commercial sites that had previously been free loading from Google's search engine to pay for AdWords. The pre-Christmas timing, so the conspiracy theorists reckoned, would leave commercial sites with little choice. Although Google undoubtedly hit established eCommerce sites there seemed to be as many winners as losers after the change, and a good many sites that were unaffected. Furthermore Google claims that there are Chinese walls between the AdWords and search parts of the organizations. Still with an IPO (Initial Public Offering) imminent there was much innuendo, especially from the people most concerned by the changes.

Optimization Filters

Another popular idea was that Google had become frustrated about the amount of highly optimized but content-light sites in its index and had implemented some kind of optimization filter. If, after analyzing on-and-off-page optimizations for a query phrase, a certain threshold was reached, the page was chucked from the results. Again the theory didn't fit well with observations as many optimized sites could still be found ranking well whereas a number of unoptimized sites had vanished. Stemming, the ability to search for derivatives of a single keyword, was introduced at around the same time as Florida and was another suspect although no-one could explain why this would affect commercial sites only.

The Austin update at the end of January 2004 made further modifications. As the changes began to settle down, and some excluded sites made their way back into the index, comment centered on Google's bag of patented technologies and whether LocalRank, Hilltop or even Topic-Sensitive PageRank algorithms had been included as part of the search. These algorithms overcome a limitation with PageRank which indicates whether a page is popular but not if it is popular for the keywords in the user's query.

CIRCA

Suspicions were also aroused by Google's acquisition of Applied Semantics along with their CIRCA technology

```
http://www.google-watch.org/circa.html
```

Ostensibly CIRCA was purchased to help the AdSense program understand the meaning of web pages. Was the technology also being used to help Google perform true content analysis?

All of these changes would require considerable computing power which is why, the experts claim, they were targeted on popular keywords with other searches being left largely untouched. It was believed that the nonsense keyword trick somehow fooled Google into not applying this filter. Google took some time to stabilize. Websites that were affected claim that the results are now less relevant but it would appear that the updates have excluded some of the most egregious examples of Black Hat SEO and search engine spam.

Whatever the exact nature of the changes the howls of pain from site owners that had predicated their business model around Google search results should serve as a lesson to others. Search engines are not under an obligation to include a particular site in their index or to go on providing high rankings especially where they feel that these damage the overall quality of the results. It is clear that pre-Florida there was a problem with relevance for many heavily targeted terms in Google's results pages. With commercial pressures from its stock market floatation and statements coming from Microsoft and Yahoo! that they would compete much more seriously in the search arena they had to react. At the same time a number of innocent sites were caught up in the chaos. Internet mavens spoke ruefully of building other traffic streams but the changes also highlighted the dangers of a mono-culture where the majority of searches go through a single provider, whether Google, Yahoo! or another.

In the wake of *Hurricane Florida* it is worth remembering the old saw that past results are no cast-iron guarantee to the future.

Post-Florida

SEO Research Labs have written an interesting report on how to prosper with the new post-Florida Google:

```
http://www.seoresearchlabs.com/seo-research-labs-google-
report.pdf
```

Freshbot and Deepbot

Google uses two robots to crawl web content, these have been dubbed the *Freshbot* and *Deepbot* after their general purpose. Deepbot is the once a month deep crawl of web content that results in the main Google index. The Freshbot crawls the Web on a continuous basis and is responsible for the Everflux effect. It finds content that is updated frequently such as news sites, forums, blogs and other websites. It appears that when Google finds a new page it checks it frequently at first to see if there are regular updates. If there are the site is added to the list of pages to be visited by the Freshbot.

The Freshbot results appear to be compiled into a separate database. This is overwritten every time the Freshbot starts a new cycle. The Freshbot and main index are merged to produce search results. The means that fresh content may appear in search results very quickly but then disappear only to resurface one or two months later in the main Google index. If the page is already in the main index the Freshbot results may appear for a few days before reverting to the older version until the site is crawled by the Deepbot.

At one time the Freshbot used internet addresses beginning with the number *64.* and Deepbot addresses beginning with *216.*; but since the middle of 2003 the Google robots all come from machines in the *64.** or *66.** address range.

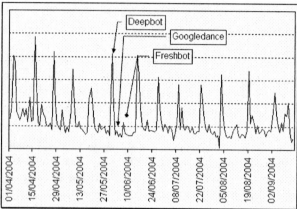

Figure 6. Google Robot Visits

Figure 6 is taken from the log files of a website; it clearly illustrates a cycle of deep crawls with a lesser number of daily visits. The Googledance follows sometime after the deep crawl as the results are processed.

G

Google

In 1998 it seemed like Silicon Valley and its dot.com phenomena was the center of the universe. At Stanford University two graduate students, Larry Page, son of a Computer Science professor at Maryland and Sergey Brin, born in Moscow to Russian parents had been working on search engine technology since they met at a conference in 1995.

At that time search engines usually relied on on-page factors to determine the ranking of web pages in their results. Searching was a bit hit-or-miss, particularly for neophytes who had trouble with advanced search forms and their arcane Boolean logic. Page and Brin developed a new way of ranking web pages based on the number of inbound-links. Effectively each inbound-link is treated as a vote for the page. Pages with more inbound-links are deemed to be more important. As a further twist the links (votes) from more important pages are also given more weight. The PageRank algorithm as a way of sifting the wheat from the chaff of search engine results was born.

The results on Stanford's computers were impressive but to launch their service Page and Brin needed venture capital to buy their own hardware and finance further development. They tried to set up a meeting with Andy Bechtolsheim, a co-founder of Sun, another successful Stanford spin-off. Bechtolsheim was interested but was a very busy man; finally they managed to grab a couple of minutes with him in a coffee shop to explain their project, now called Google.

Bechtolsheim immediately offered a check for 100,000 dollars, *"we'll work out the details later..."*, he told them before rushing off to another meeting. There was one big problem, the check was made out to Google Inc., a company that did not yet exist. Fortunately just the rumor that Bechtolsheim had given money was enough to get other venture capitalists running in Google's direction. Brin and Page had originally wanted to call the company *googol*, a term that means ten to the power of one hundred. However the domain name googol.com had already been registered in April, 1995.

Google was launched out of a building in Menlo Park, California on the 7th of September 1998. The Googleplex was born. In addition to Bechtolsheim's initial seed money the pair raised a further $1 million dollars. The following summer two investment capital funds would put up another $25 million.

At a time when other search engines were polluting their results with paid inclusion and sponsored links and wrapping the search interface inside a *portal* news of Google spread rapidly, especially amongst computer geeks. By the late spring of 2000 Google was answering 18 million queries each day and had become the biggest search engine on the Web. The interface was incredibly simple - just text box, but thanks to PageRank the results were amazingly good, invariably pulling up the requested information or website in the top ten links. Google often indexed the mass of information that had appeared on company websites better than their internal search interface. This ease of use meant that it was becoming a firm favorite with the increasingly large number of non-expert users on the Web. So much so that the term *googling for information* has entered the lexicon. In a major coup Yahoo!, the largest website around, decided to use Google to supply its own search results.

Technology

Google has sought to extend the reach of its technology to include news sources, weblogs and personal email. The introduction of Gmail proved controversial with privacy campaigners who believe that indexing personal email represents an intrusion of privacy. Google's *Froogle (frugal* - groan!*)* search engine provides price comparisons for users searching for products. Google is built using off the shelf PC hardware configured in a cluster of over 10,000 machines (some people think they have closer to 50,000 machines) running a customized version of the Linux operating system. On the same day that Microsoft announced the beta launch of its new algorithmic search engine Google doubled the number of pages in their index to a claimed 8 billion. Some of these pages may not be fully indexed and return results based only on URL and title keywords. The update showed that Google was capable of rolling out changes to its massive array of computers and that it was not afraid to play the marketing game with Microsoft.

Content Targeted Advertising

For a long time Google resisted the urge to go public. The leitmotif for the company is *"never do anything evil"*. While some people question this the company is viewed a lot more favorably than that other behemoth of computing, Microsoft. Google concentrated on building up revenue streams, from selling its search technology to the more recent introduction of the AdWords and AdSense programs. The former lets websites bid on keywords; winners have a small advert placed on the same page as relevant search results or on pages of partners in the AdSense program. Overall this form of unobtrusive advertising has been well received although some Web users run blocker software on their browser. Post IPO Google posted a doubling of profits and revenues both of which show strong growth due to online advertising.

Before Yahoo! switched to its own results early in 2004 it was estimated that Google's total share of web searches was close to 80% because, in addition to Yahoo!, Google supplies results to AOL, AskJeeves and Alexa.

IPO

Google's much anticipated IPO, while trying to stay true to the company's philosophy, attracted a lot of criticism, especially from pundits. Rather than go down the traditional IPO route with an investment bank issuing a limited number of shares to selected clients who then make a killing on a first day bounce in the share price, Google decided to stage an auction. First of all Google discovered that it may have illegally issued staff with shares, it then had to raise the allocation of shares following the settlement of a patent lawsuit with Yahoo! concerning the AdWords technology. The run up to the launch is supposed to be a quiet period but Google ran foul of the Securities and Exchange Commission after an interview with the founders was published in Playboy magazine. Finally the company was forced to scale back the offering and reduce the target share price. In the end things went better than expected with the shares opening at just over $100 on the 19th August, 2004. An 18% increase on the offer price.

Competition

The main threat to Google is probably Microsoft which intends to include search technology in the next release of its operating system, codenamed Longhorn, in 2006. Microsoft's search technology will seamlessly integrate local and remote search on a computer (firms such as Blinx.com already offer this if users download a small piece of software). Remote searches will be supported by Microsoft's search engine. In a bid to preempt Microsoft and other competitors Google has recently launched a preview of their own Desktop Search Tool <http://desktop.google.com/>. This widget presents desktop search as another Google tab. Currently only Internet Explorer and Windows XP and 2000 with service pack 3 are supported. It seems particularly good at indexing Microsoft documents, prying inside password protected files. The results are presented just like normal Google search results and it can even show cached versions of files and thread messages and emails. As with Gmail the tool has raised concerns about privacy, especially the mixing of local and remote search results.

Microsoft Search has recently undergone a revamp which Microsoft claims will make it a Google killer. The relevance of results obtained early in the beta test was somewhat disappointing but they have slowly improved. It will be interesting to see just how many security problems integrated search introduces to Microsoft's operating system and whether Google Desktop Search can overcome its own privacy issues. Still with effective control over the majority of desktop operating systems Microsoft is a serious competitor even if early versions of their products turn out to be mediocre.

Optimizing for Google

Because Google is currently so important for search many people spend a great deal of time trying to figure out how it works. Beyond the PageRank patent little is known for certain although a mass of empirical evidence has allowed many optimizers to achieve very good rankings for their sites in the face of better funded competition.

Practically everyone knows about PageRank these days. Even *The Economist* has published a detailed explanation for the benefit of the MBAs. Apart from PageRank Google says that it uses over 100 other factors in ranking web pages. Currently anchor text in inbound-links is very important. Good inbound-links with relevant anchor text can easily take a site to number one. On-page factors are less important as the Google engineers feel these are too easy to manipulate but relevant Title and Heading elements should be used. For less competitive combinations of keywords a single factor such as matching Title element may place a page in the top ten results. This can lead some users astray, believing they have stumbled upon the silver bullet of search engine optimization.

In an effort to confound SEO experts and provide better results Google is constantly tinkering with its algorithms and has also developed technology such as Hilltop and LocalRank that may be used to refine the PageRank process and make it hard to use Black Hat techniques to spam pages into high rankings. Google makes small changes very often. Sometimes a new algorithm will be trialed on a set of users on a particularly Internet sub-network before being rolled out or modified.

The Googledance

The Googledance is Google's time of the month. The dance is a major re-ranking of web pages that occurs after the Deepbot has finished indexing content. It manifests itself in fluctuating site positions in search results and changes in an individual site's toolbar rank. It is a time of great excitement for site owners as their sites gain or lose toolbar rank.

The Google dance is unannounced but can be detected when results between the various data centers that Google serves results from are out of synch. These were traditionally: www1, www2 and www3.google.com. However since the IPO Google has become much more protective of its operation and these data centers are no longer publicly visible except through their IP addresses. McDar has a tool that can compare results between these new data centers:

```
http://www.mcdar.net/dance/index.php
```

The traditional Googledance has been less regular since the Florida Update although Google watchers have noticed lots of fluctuation in rankings as a result of algorithm changes. During the summer of 2004 the toolbar ranking went about 3 months without being updated even though site rankings did change regularly during this period.

Google's Beauty Pageant

You may be wondering which the top ranking sites in the Google database are. There is an easy way to find out, just enter the query *http* and Google will return the first 1000 sites in its index. If you use SEO Chat's PageRank search

```
http://www.seochat.com/seo-tools/pagerank-search
```

you will notice that the results don't always follow the Google toolbar PageRank, another indication that PageRank is not the only factor in Google ranking.

Googleblog

Google has started a weblog which can give some useful insights into search and other services:

```
http://www.google.com/googleblog/
```

H

Hidden Pages

Be careful about the almost divine ability of search engines to ferret out pages on your website. This is especially important if you are hosting the site on an in-house server.

There are a number of mechanisms whereby search engines can find such pages. If someone looks at your hidden pages then surfs to another site the URL of the hidden page will be in the site's log file. If this is accessible to a search engine robot it will eventually follow this referrer link to your hidden pages.

Some toolbars and browsers like Opera communicate the addresses of pages that they visit to search engines. The engine may then dispatch a robot to index those pages.

The sort of information that search engines find can range from new versions of the website, to private documents, to security information on the host server. This can include website administration scripts, the server's password files or even credit card details stored on an eCommerce server.

Hilltop Algorithm

The Hilltop algorithm was proposed by two researchers working under the auspices of the University of Toronto. One of those researchers is now at Google and Google also acquired the patent early in 2003. The algorithm overcomes problems with broad search terms which return large sets of documents that have to be ranked. It is hard for a search engine to analyze the quality of these results based on on-page factors alone, especially where the results are heavily optimized for search engines or are copies of other high ranking pages.

The Hilltop algorithm is based on a similar assumption to Google PageRank. That is the quality and quantity of inbound-links is an indication of how the page should be ranked. The key difference is that only *"expert sources"* derived from the query terms are used when judging inbound-links. In other words Google's original PageRank algorithm gives a global rank of the quality of a web page. Hilltop determines the quality based on the relevance to the query term.

Expert or Authority Sites

An expert or authority page covers a certain topic based on the query text and has links to many none-affiliated pages on the same topic area. An example would be an Open Directory Project (DMOZ) or Yahoo! directory page. Search results are only considered if they have more than one inbound-link from these expert pages and those inbound-links contain anchor text that matches the target page and the query terms. If Hilltop can't find more than one expert page it returns no results. The algorithm is oriented towards quality not quantity of results.

To score highly under Hilltop sites have to acquire inbound-links from expert sites. This can be by writing articles or providing other useful information. These can be placed on the website and possibly submitted to authority sites with a link request.

Sites are judged to be affiliated if they are on the same Internet network (using IP address information) or the same domain. This should help to exclude link farms.

The exact implementation of Hilltop is described in Bharat and Mihaila's paper:

```
http://www.cs.toronto.edu/~georgem/hilltop/
```

It is believed by some experts to form a significant part of Google's Florida algorithm changes that penalized many heavily optimized and commercial web pages. An obvious problem is the compilation of the expert pages and the processing necessary to match with results pages. It seems likely that the Hilltop algorithm is only run on certain popular keywords with a precompiled set of expert pages.

I

Inbound Links

An inbound-link (IBL) is any hypertext link from an external website to a page on your site. In the Google universe the terms backlinks or backward links are often used. The ability to click on a piece of text and see a related page is a fundamental part of what makes the World Wide Web useful. For an individual website owner inbound-links are important for the following reasons:

- They can increase your ranking in search engine results pages for queries using the keywords in the link anchor text.

- Inbound-links from a site already indexed by a search engine will enable the robot to find your site during the normal indexing process. Each inbound-link represents a possible entry point to your website, increasing the frequency and depth of indexing.

- They can increase your site's PageRank or ranking with similar algorithms.

- They bring extra traffic to your site.

The first two benefits are probably the most significant. PageRank is a key component of the Google search engine but it has been diluted by recent algorithm changes. If you have created a content rich, authority site for your keywords, inbound-links will trickle in naturally as webmasters link to your pages.

However it is a bit of a Catch-22 situation because inbound-links and especially their associated anchor text count as a major element in site rankings. Webmasters looking for interesting content to link to may have difficulty finding your site until there is sufficient inbound-link density. As many webmasters' knowledge of SEO doesn't extend beyond the Google Toolbar PageRank figure they are often reluctant to link to brand new PR0 pages for fear of diluting the ranking of their own site. Commercial sites such as online shops find it even harder to get inbound-links through organic growth. Adding customer reviews and detailed product information can be one method to attract inbound-links. These natural links are probably the most valuable. They will use varied anchor text and will usually come from relevant, content rich pages with few outbound-links. They also don't require a reciprocal link.

Getting listed in a search engine can in itself be a struggle. Some engines let you submit links for free with no guarantee of when your site will be indexed. Others require a payment, especially for rapid submission. There are even engines that seem to have no obvious means of submitting new sites. However a single link from a site already in the search engine's index is usually the fastest way of getting listed with the advantage of costing nothing.

Press Releases

One traditional method of at least making people aware of your shiny new website is to write a press release. This should mention the website's URL, contact details and give some interesting information about the site and products. Linked with a promotion it could get some publicity from eZines, related websites, forums and blogs. Use search engines to find related sites that use your target keywords and send your release to the press contact or webmaster.

Cross-Linking

Perhaps the simplest method of getting inbound-links is cross-linking with other sites. Use the above method as the starting point for finding other sites to contact. Cross-linking has fallen into disrepute with some SEO experts of late. In terms of PageRank it rarely has better than a neutral impact and unscrupulous sites can implement schemes to hoard their PageRank. Excessive cross-links, especially with unrelated sites, may even be indistinguishable from a link farm and could be a component in getting a site banned. Compared to natural links in content pages, lists of links rarely feed more than a trickle of visitors. However they can be a source of keyword rich anchor text and can direct search engines into the site.

Relevant Anchor Text

Relevant anchor text is probably one of the main areas where inbound-links fail to live up to their potential. You should provide potential link partners with the anchor text and description that you would like them to use when linking to your site. Otherwise the link will often just be some version of the domain name. Don't hesitate to ask people linking to your site to modify the anchor text. This should ideally correspond to the content of the page being linked to and should target the main keywords.

Web Directories

Directories can be an important source of inbound-links. The Open Directory Project <DMOZ: http://www.dmoz.org/> and Yahoo! are two examples of themed directories. Look up the category that corresponds most closely to your site's contents. These directories are also a source of much frustration as suggestions can take many months, if ever, to be included. DMOZ is particularly chaotic in some areas as it relies on the goodwill of volunteer editors. Both directories provide a boost to PageRank, although this can be spread quite thinly over a large number of outgoing links and both guarantee that the site will also get spidered by the Google and Yahoo! search engines. There are many other directories ranging from general to trade to local lists. These can be found through Google or Yahoo! by searching for: *keyword(s) directory*.

This raises another question, is a good PR6 inbound-link with no relevant anchor text (the ubiquitous: *click here* springs to mind) better than a PR5 link with relevant anchor text? Given that the PageRank shown on the Google Toolbar is a non-linear scale (each jump in PR is worth something like 8 times more than the previous level) it may still be worth going for the PR6 link as it will be possible to distribute its effects through internal links, all with good, keyword rich, anchor text.

Another source of potential inbound-links is from sites that link to your competitors. Most search engines support the *link* query operator to show inbound-links. On Google this is actually a bit misleading as it includes internal links and excludes many backlinks that are less than PR4. Use Yahoo! to get a better picture.

Wikis, Blogs and Forums

Wikis, user editable websites, can be a rich vein to tap for inbound-links. They often have good PageRank but avoid spamming them, only link where you have good, relevant content. Some SEO Experts also suggest contributing to forums, newsgroups and blog comments. The value of incoming links is often negligible (especially for *signature* URLs) and they usually represent less worth than the effort to write a post. They can generate click-throughs and get your website better known in the community. Remember that the rules of the forum or blog should also be respected unless you want to get a bad reputation and suffer possible repercussions. If your site has valuable content search out any on-line FAQs (Frequently Asked Questions) on the subject and suggest a link to the FAQ maintainer.

Another technique for generating inbound-link is to provide some useful tool or service that can be integrated into other sites. An obvious example is a piece of web software or tool that has a link back to your site. This is how many producers of Blog software have such great PageRanks. Web Services are an ideal way of making information available to third parties.

A lot of eCommerce sites generate traffic and a significant number of inbound-links through affiliate programs. These give a percentage of each sale or lead the affiliate site makes in return for promoting your products. The eCommerce site will normally use an external company to manage their affiliate program. Inbound-links contain special codes that tell the affiliate manager where the traffic is coming from. The Google AdWords program can also be used with some success to generate traffic from sites with content relevant to the target keywords.

Buying Links

Because inbound-links are such a key feature of many search engines' ranking methodology schemes that artificially and unnaturally boost the number of such links are a target for penalty and possible bans. Buying links from highly ranked sites is particularly frowned upon. Often these sites spread their PageRank over so many outbound-links that they represent little value to the purchaser.

Internal Links

Internal links are hyperlinks that join the documents in your website. This is assuming you have more than one page which should be the case if you are serious about optimizing your site. You have direct control over these internal links so this is the place to start using the keywords that you are targeting in anchor text. It is possible to beat much better PageRanked sites using a combination of internal links with relevant anchor text and good, well structured, content. Now the alert reader may be thinking after reading the section about Anchor Text that content isn't really that necessary. That's not the case. You have to consider how long a user will spend exploring your site if there is little or no content on the first page they come to. In web marketing jargon the site is said to not be *sticky*. If you want to go up against content rich, highly page ranked sites you will need to use every weapon in the SEO armory. It all counts, even if just a little.

If you already have good, keyword rich content then the obvious place to start is to make links from those keywords to relevant pages on your own site. The key for long term success is not to do anything that will adversely affect the readability or navigability of your pages. Similar rules for keyword density can be applied to anchor text density; anywhere from 1 - 20% of your keywords can be internal links. You should avoid excessive repetition of the same anchor keywords on a single page. By mixing and matching both anchor keywords and targets you can cover a number of keyword variations and target different, relevant content on your site. Do this for enough pages and you will soon have a number of good anchors for each page on your site. From a search engine's viewpoint your site will look like a set of content rich and well linked pages and not some kind of attempt to subvert their search algorithms. Just what your visitors are looking for.

If you are responsible for creating new content, or mentoring the people who will, try to get into the habit of interlinking as you write. After a while this will come naturally. These links add value for search engines and more especially for your readers who can follow their own path through your content. This is the original aim of hypertext.

Image Links

Many web authoring/site management tools, such as Microsoft FrontPage, will create standard menu bars (navigation maps) linking to subordinate pages and to the home page. These should also use consistent and relevant anchor text. Where you want text to say one thing and yet give a different message you can do this with an image. An example would be a site logo that appears on each page. This is done using the ALT attribute of the HTML IMG element:

```
<a href="index.htm"><img ="logo.gif" alt="search engine
optimization"></a>
```

The ALT attribute is indexed by all the major search engines where it is part of an anchor element. This way each page links back to the site's home page with the targeted keywords.

Home Page

The focus of most websites is the home or root index page. This usually has the most value to search engines, either because they index this page more frequently or because it carries the most inbound-links. As well as the standard navigational structure there are usually opportunities for deep linking into the site using keyword rich anchor text. Here a site map can help. A large site will cover a number of subject areas each with its own index page and similar rules to the homepage apply.

Hyperlink TITLE Attributes

Anchor tags may also include a TITLE attribute. This should correspond to the title of the target page and may be used by the browser to pop up a *tool-tip* style dialog showing the information. It is not currently indexed by any of the search engines.

J

Jump Pages

It is difficult to cover all your keyword bases in a single page, optimize for various search engine algorithms and keep the text coherent for human readers. A common solution is to create alternative versions of the same page. These pages go under many names, *Doorway, Hallway, Bridge, Gateway* and *Entry Pages* are often bandied about, especially by SEO businesses, often to obfuscate their intentions.

At their simplest Jump Pages are targeted at a few keywords and designed purely to rank well in search engines. A user clicking on the page will be presented with some hyperlink text inviting him into the rest of the site. Porn sites pioneered and continue to use this technique. A user may search for the name of an actress, the page features the name of the actress repeated many times usually interspersed with other words such as *nude* and *pictures*. The page then has links to adult content sites, although rarely featuring the aforementioned lady. Okay I know what you are thinking but it is a tough job and someone has to check this stuff. This is a classic bait and switch tactic.

The problem with this is that it is all too obvious to end users. The conversion rate is not going to be very high and sites using this technique have to rely on quantity, creating thousands of doorways. It is also easy for competitors to see the successful pages and copy the techniques with few or little changes. Duplicate page algorithms mean that many of the copied doorways will be dropped from the search engine index.

Meta Refresh

The first improvement to the basic scheme is to use a META Refresh tag with a zero second delay. This is the jump. The user probably won't be able to see the optimized content before being sent elsewhere. These META tags are also a red flag to search engines that something may be wrong with the page. Because jump pages manipulate results and clutter indexes with redundant text they are banned by search engines. TrafficPower, a major SEO firm used a technique called *Search Engine Entry Pages* that they claimed would get clients into Google's Top Ten but allegedly ended up getting their clients banned from both Google and Yahoo!

JavaScript Redirects and TrafficPower

Other tactics for redirecting users while leaving search engine robots to index the optimized content have been developed. The aim, as ever, is to keep at least one step ahead of the experts at the search engine companies. One example is the use of JavaScript, a popular web programming language. Search engines don't understand JavaScript, building this knowledge into search engine robots would make them too complicated and slow. JavaScript can be used to load a fresh page when a certain action occurs. TrafficPower used JavaScript *onmouseover()* events to trigger the redirect.

Microsoft

Some sharp eyed surfers discovered that Microsoft was using doorway pages for certain parts of its website. The pages contained densely formatted, keyword rich text that was obviously not designed to be read by humans. Each page included a function in an external JavaScript file:

```
function balise(s, ids, idt) {
  var asp = 'http://msasia.domain255.com/img.asp?l=|' +
  navigator.userLanguage + '|&r=|' + document.referrer + '|&s=|'
  + ids + '|&t=|' + idt + '|&g=' + s;
  location.replace(asp);
}
```

At the head of the page a call was made to the function with the following code:

```
<SCRIPT language="JavaScript">

balise("http://www.microsoft.com/asia/solutionmarketplace/soluti
on.asp?ind=6&sid=60101&type=1&sLanguage=14", "33", "462");
</SCRIPT>
```

The key part is the call to *location.replace(URL)* which loads the new contents. As a final protection the doorway page includes a directive telling search engines not to archive the keyword rich content.

```
<META name="ROBOTS" content="NOARCHIVE">
```

The pages had been created by an SEO company. French holiday firm VVF <http://www.hiver.vvf-vacances.fr> also used this service. The discovery of these pages has led people to ask why, if TrafficPower and its clients got banned from Google for similar tactics, why not Microsoft?

This illustrates a few points

- Jump pages obviously do work if people found the sites mentioned through these doorways. However there are better and less risky ways to optimize your site.

- What constitutes a breach of a search engine's terms and conditions is a gray area.

- A search engine may have difficulty detecting examples of Black Hat SEO.

- Search engines can be completely arbitrary in who they ban. Google probably feels that it would degrade their search engine to ban a content rich site such as Microsoft's.

Just be aware of the risks and limitations of using doorway pages.

Jump pages implemented with JavaScript redirects are fairly easy for humans to detect even if they cause current search engine robots some trouble. A more advanced scheme is agent name delivery or cloaking which delivers content at the server level customized to different audiences.

Some black-hatters make the point that every page on a website is a doorway or entry page and that separating search engine optimized content actually enhances the user experience. There are reasons for using doorways, for example, to enable content that cannot be indexed by robots to be found. An example would be information held in a database. This could be exported to static pages with a link to a page enabling the database to be searched dynamically. There are usually better ways to achieve this than jump pages.

As we have seen with TrafficPower and other SEO firms, jump pages are a mainstay of many optimization tactics even though changes to a search engine's algorithms can make them much less effective. Beware of over inflated claims such as guaranteed top ten listings for competitive search terms:

```
To: webmaster@mydomain.com
Subject: 300+ Optimized Doorway Pages to YOUR Website!!

Are you still using just ONE web site to compete for Internet
business? Imagine owning 300 individual web pages indexed to all
of the major web bots.

Now imagine that every one of them is designed with a different
keyword order and keyword density. Imagine those keywords are
your keywords.

New technology makes well known search engine BLITZ technique
available to all web businesses!! NO HOSTING CHARGE FOR 300
PAGES!

Take advantage of...
THOUSANDS OF KEYWORD COMBINATIONS - YOUR KEYWORDS!
RANDOMIZED TITLE AND BODY TAGS
300 OPTIMIZED PAGES
....ALL SPIDERED TO THE 53 MAJOR SEARCH ENGINES
...ALL POINTING TO YOU!!!

Learn more about BLITZING the search engines!!!
```

WebPosition Gold

Many of these businesses use software packages to machine generate pages. An example of such a package is WebPosition Gold <www.web-positiongold.com/> (WPG). This package features a template that the webmaster fills in with target keywords and other text. The Page Generator then creates pages that are supposed to be tailored for different search engines predilections for on-page ranking factors. The process is quite scientific using statistical analysis of which on-page factors a search engine prefers. So far so bad but as many people find after an algorithm update, today's top ranking pages are tomorrow's turkeys. Machine generated pages, especially ones using gibberish as filler text, are usually easier for search engines to detect and ban. Finally, most search engines put less reliance on on-page factors.

Creating a Jump Page

To give you a better idea of the process we will create a jump page by hand. There's no magic and no need for expensive software. You can use a tool such as Overture's keyword suggestions generator

```
http://inventory.overture.com/d/searchinventory/suggestion/
```

For this exercise we will target the term SEO. Overture gives a list of alternative keyword phrases and the frequency that they were queried in the previous month. For our term we got a list of about 100 phrases. We'll use the top ten, although one could include the whole list.

```
9897 seo company
7202 seo services
4619 seo optimization
4133 seo expert
3670 seo firm
2528 seo tool
2250 seo service
2048 seo web site
1989 seo consultant
1957 seo training
```

By cutting and pasting the list into Excel or Word the count column can be deleted leaving a list of phrases.

```
seo company
seo services
seo optimization
seo expert
seo firm
seo tool
seo service
seo web site
seo consultant
seo training
```

A page consisting of just these terms would look a bit odd and would probably trigger some keyword stuffing filters on search engines. They need to be mixed up with some other text to give a keyword density of around 20%. If you are a dab hand at programming, a simple Perl script could be used to generate the content using any text as the source.

```
Once more seo company into the breach, seo services. Or close
the seo optimization wall up with our English seo expert In
```

```
peace there's nothing so becomes a seo firm As modest seo tool
and humility; But when the blast of seo service blows in our
ears, Then imitate the action of the seo web site; Stiffen the
sinews, summon up the seo consultant, Disguise fair nature with
hard-favor'd seo training;
```

Here we've used part of Shakespeare's Henry Vth as source text. It is out of copyright. Around 300 - 600 words with the list of phrases repeated some 5 to 10 times should do and each phrase should be included in Headers and the Title. It would also be worth generating some hyperlinks with strong anchors through to different pages on the site. Of course the text makes no sense to a human reader but a search engine would have to perform some pretty good semantic analysis to know that.

Remember that jump pages can get your site banned so do this at your risk and peril.

K

Keywords

Keywords (sometimes abbreviated to kw) are the words that users type into a search engine when looking for information on a certain subject area. For example entering the term:

vintage motorbikes

into a search engine should return a set of results that link to pages relevant to the keywords. The search engine uses a mixture of different algorithms to ensure the results are as accurate as possible. SEO experts will research the most common keywords related to a page's contents and will then alter on-page and off-page factors in order to ensure high rankings for those keywords.

Each page on the website should target a small set of keywords related to the page content. Large, generic pages should be split up. The home page of the site generally has the most inbound links and should concentrate on the most competitive keywords.

In reality it is not quite such an all or nothing process. Targeting generic terms will still provide some weight for more specific terms. For example the single keyword *computer* will also target derivatives such as *laptop computer* and *computer software services*, although given two identical pages search engines will give a higher rank to more specific keywords. At the same time more specific keywords will dilute the value for other combinations. Thus a site targeting *computer software services* will rank less well than one targeting *computer software* for the query term *computer software engineering*. It is a case of swings and roundabouts. Pages deep in a website should be much more focused on specific content and keywords. Focusing on more specific keywords, highly relevant to the content should also give more stable site rankings during algorithm updates such as Google's Florida. Although they will only attract niche traffic these should be better qualified visitors leading to more sales. Adjacency is also an important factor, search engines assign more rank to pages where search terms occur next to each other.

Popularity and Competition

It is worth being realistic about keyword choices. Keywords with up to 100,000 pages indexed Google or Yahoo! should be fairly easy to rank for with some basic search engine optimization. Up to a million pages and a high ranking will require inbound links coupled with relevant anchor text along with factors directly under the website owner's control: site structure, on-page optimizations, content and page count. Above a million indexed pages and any ranking in results pages gets exponentially more difficult and may well be beyond the resources of a small website. You can think of keywords as mountains. It may be more worthwhile to climb a large number of smaller peaks than try to scale Everest and fail.

Accidental Keywords

The above is just a rough guide. There are queries featuring popular keywords but in odd combinations that can return huge numbers of results but a lot of these are accidental. Most of the websites are not competing for these keywords. A site that is optimized for the exact phrase can feature in the top ten relatively easily. This technique is sometimes used by search engine optimizers to show that they can rank highly for *competitive* search terms.

The number of pages indexed by search engines for a particular keyword combination is irrelevant if no-one is searching for those words. A good example is the phrase *click here*, this returns around 40 million pages in Google but very few people search on this term (although some do!). Overture:

```
http://inventory.overture.com/d/searchinventory/suggestion/
```

and Wordtracker:

```
http://www.wordtracker.com
```

provide tools to help optimize keywords. There are some meta-tools on the Web that enable a user to consult both these resources from a single web page:

```
http://www.digitalpoint.com/tools/suggestion/
```

They give the popularity of keyword combinations and also suggest alternative keywords. Google provides a keyword alternatives tool:

```
https://www.adwords.google.com/select/KeywordSandbox
```

based on data from their AdWords program. A number of search engines also show which the current most popular keywords are, Google's Zeitgeist breaks this information down geographically:

```
http://www.google.com/press/zeitgeist.html
```

Rankings and Click-Throughs

Figure 7 shows an analysis of some of the most popular keywords from the log files of a website. These keywords occupied positions 1 to 10 in Google search engine results pages. Looking up the popularity of the keywords in Overture and comparing with the number of Google searches arriving at the site enables a conversion rate to be plotted against the position in the search results. For example if 1000 people per day search on the keyword(s) and the site is in first position for the search in Google the site could expect 800 visitors for that keyword. If the site is in position two the figure drops to around 600 and in position 10 closer to 200. Only 15% of searchers make it beyond the first twenty results. The graph is for illustration only as it is based on a fairly limited sample size.

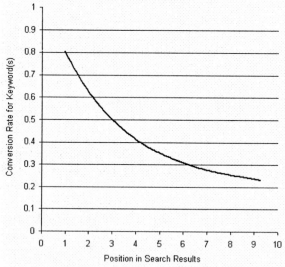

Figure 7. Keyword click-throughs plotted against position in search results

Achieving a high ranking in a search engine for a single keyword is hardest as there are also more potential competitors. The OneStat survey:

http://www.onestat.com

shows that two and three keyword searches are currently the most popular amongst searchers. The trend is towards using more keywords in searches showing a greater sophistication amongst users. This implies that pages should be optimized for two and three keyword queries. Here keyword proximity (or adjacency) is a factor as exact matches are given more weight.

Keyword Effectiveness Index (KEI)

Keywords vary in competitiveness. Table 2 gives five computer related keywords with the number of pages indexed in Google, Yahoo! and MSN Search.

Keyword	Google	Yahoo!	MSN Search	CBA
computer	234.0 M	252.0 M	53.0 M	1.68
laptop computer	9.0 M	10.5 M	2.2 M	3.11
personal computer	14.2 M	52.4 M	11.1 M	0.10
apple computer	7.0 M	18.2 M	3.8 M	0.61
computer keyboard	5.4 M	9.9 M	1.9 M	0.21

Table 2. Keyword Competition and Popularity

The figure in the final column is a cost/benefit analysis (CBA). Wordtracker uses the term *Keyword Effectiveness Index* or KEI and offers a tool called *Competition Search* to calculate this value. This tool may be useful if you have a lot of keyword combinations to check. The disadvantage is that you have to pay to use it. *Competition Search* uses a database of search queries and matches these against the total results for the query in popular search engines to give a measure of how popular and completive a keyword is.

It is possible to calculate the CBA figure by hand using query data either from Wordtracker or Overture. The figure was obtained by taking the number of people searching for the keyword over a month as reported by Overture and dividing it by the total number of web pages indexed by Google, currently the most popular search engine. The table illustrates that certain keywords are easier to target than others for the same traffic. In theory the higher the CBA value the better but this makes three big assumptions:

1. The competitiveness of a keyword is proportional to the number of pages in the index. Except for some odd keywords like "*home page*" this is probably fairly reasonable.

2. For the same number of clicks, all keywords have the same value to a website owner. This is almost certainly inaccurate. Users searching for "*apple computer*" may account for more sales revenue than those looking for "*computer keyboard*".

3. The conversion rate is constant. This is not the case. Qualified traffic is more valuable than general traffic. An Apple computer dealer will covert proportionally more people searching for "*apple computer*" than "*computer*" into sales. An Apple computer dealer that is based in San Francisco with no mail order outlet will make more sales on "*apple computer store San Francisco*" than just "*apple computer*".

Optimizers should also remember that many keywords are seasonal or related to specific events. For example the number of users searching for anything related to the Olympics peaks every four years, summer holidays in late winter and recipes for turkey around Thanksgiving.

Optimization

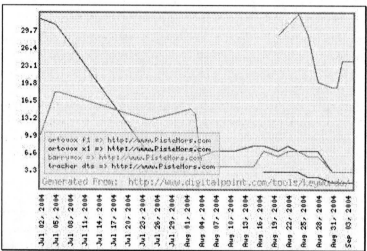

Figure 8. Keywords Targeted as part of an eCommerce campaign

Once a set of keywords has been researched for a page the final step is to use them in the anchor text of inbound and internal links, the page URL, the page TITLE element, headings and also within the page copy itself. Optimizers should avoid keyword stuffing or *spamdexing* on the page.

Search Engine Optimization is a continuous process. Keywords should be tracked in the various search engines. This can be done through custom scripts using the Google-API or by online tools. Digital Point:

```
http://www.digitalpoint.com/tools/keywords/
```

offers a Google keyword tracking tool on their website which can be used as part of a campaign to show the effectiveness of keyword optimizations or as part of long term tracking to ensure any problems are flagged up in a timely manner.

Multimedia

Many search engines are capable of indexing multimedia including images, Adobe PDF files and Microsoft Office documents. Use keyword rich file names as these formats can bring in visitors. It is possible to set the title of Office documents and PDF files which should further optimize the content. The main problem with images searches are that the visitors are not well qualified and often don't stay long on the site.

Keyword Density

Keyword density is the percentage of target keywords relative to the total text on a page. It is where Search Engine Optimization strategies were at a few years back. Readers may remember getting suckered into doorway pages where keywords were repeated hundreds of times in the page title and body text. Because keyword density is an on-page factor it is too easy for website owners to manipulate so it carries much less weight with search engines nowadays.

Checking the top ten pages for popular search terms using a keyword density analysis tool:

```
http://www.keyworddensity.com/
```

reveals densities ranging from zero to around 15% for the body text. The only place where keyword density plays a significant role is for searches for uncompetitive keywords. Website owners should concentrate on writing good, themed copy rather than trying to fulfill a certain quota of keywords on a page.

Keyword Stuffing

Keyword stuffing is the excessive use of keywords in either the text of a page or within certain *hidden* HTML elements. In particular the Page Title, image Alternative Text (ALT), hidden Form fields and Meta tags are all candidates for keyword stuffing as they are not directly visible to the end user but may be indexed by search engines. In response to keyword stuffing, search engines have improved their algorithms to detect the excessive use of keywords or to only use keyword information in conjunction with other factors such as hyperlinks. Keyword stuffing can even get a website banned; this is usually through a competitor reporting the site for overloading or spamming.

L

Link Farms

Link farms are sites that link to one another with the sole intent of boosting link popularity. Because Google dislikes links between unrelated content some Link Farms have divided their links into categories, much like the Yahoo! directory. Well a real farmer wouldn't mix his beans, apples and maize in the same field would he? In return for including your link in the farm you agree to download and host somewhere on your website all the other links in the category. This must be done on a page that is reachable by search engine spiders and the page must be updated on a regular basis to include new links. An example of this type of link program is the *LinksToYou.com* farm.

The problem from a search engine viewpoint is that these link pages don't provide any real benefit to users while at the same time skewing the results returned by search engines. Using link farms is strictly forbidden by the leading search engine's terms and conditions. The problem for search engines is differentiating between a link farm and other types of content. In the case of the most notorious link farms simply placing an outbound link to the farm or its clients may result in a ban. The link pages generated by some link programs can also have characteristics and HTML code that may be identified by the search engines.

Some webmasters have rolled their own link farms. These consist of multiple domains with lots of cross linking in the hope that it will fool the search engines into thinking that the sites are popular. Where the cross linking is between domains hosted on web servers that are physically close, that is the last three numbers in an Internet address are the same:

```
121.100.168.2
121.100.168.27
```

then these are referred to as affiliated sites and search engine algorithms may discount the links.

You will often receive unsolicited email inviting you to take part in link farm schemes:

```
Dear Webmaster,
```

```
I just visited your site and thought that it would make an
excellent affiliate link partner with our site. To get started,
just click on the link below and follow the instructions.

http://www.link-farm.com/cgi-bin/signup.cgi

Respectfully,

Rebecca,
```

It may sound like a tempting, no-effort way to create inbound links but it could result in your site being banned from the major search engines and the links will bring no benefit to your readers. Usually the inbound-links you will receive will be on low ranked sites and any PageRank will be divided over dozens of outbound-links.

LocalRank

LocalRank is another piece of Google technology. It holds US patent number 6,725,259, granted on the 20th April 2004 to Krishna Bharat. Bharat is also one of the researchers behind the Hilltop algorithm. The process is relatively simple. An initial set of results is found based on search keywords. These results are then ranked according to their interconnectivity. This has the implication that the content of the interlinked documents is related and should exclude the simplest forms of cross-linking and link-spamming. It has been suggested that LocalRank forms a part of the Florida/Austin update, perhaps using a corpus of 1000 results from the initial keyword search. However there is no confirmation of this.

The implication of LocalRank is that SEOs will now have to find inbound-links from related authority sites, directories and even from direct competitors rather than just concentrating on link quantity and anchor text. This will require a greater understanding of clients and their market segments rather than SEO tricks. Effort should be expanded in finding thematic portals and directories. For competitive keywords LocalRank favors larger, well structured informational sites with excellent content and strongly themed inbound-links.

M

Misspellings

To err is human, and all too common it would seem. For example Google ran a project to analyze misspellings of the first name of Britney Spears, a singer, over a three month period from information provided by their spelling correction system:

```
http://www.google.com/jobs/britney.html
```

Over 20% of the queries were incorrectly spelt with the two most common errors, *brittany* and *brittney*, covering around 16% of searches. Assuming people don't accept the correction suggested by Google or Yahoo! that is an awful lot of searches going somewhere. Britney Spears may not the easiest name to spell, there is an urban legend that her parents named her after the province of Brittany in Western France where they had once taken a vacation but didn't know how to spell the name correctly.

Not all errors are misspellings. Some are good old fashioned typos; these commonly involve forgotten letters and reversed letter pairs in a word. Examples are *traslation* instead of *translation* and *eihgt* instead of *eight*.

Domain Names

There are two ways we can use misspellings. We can register domains for misspellings of popular keywords, brands and existing domain names in the hope of piggy-backing off other people's SEO efforts. This borders on cyber-squatting and is strictly a Black Hat technique. This also has the corollary that if we are going to invest money establishing a domain name we should also consider registering common misspellings in addition to registering in different countries to protect our brand. This can begin to cost quite a bit of money in registration fees and is only worthwhile for well funded sites.

As an example, common misspellings of the domain: *google.com* are *gogle.com*, *googel.com* and *goolge.com*. All of these redirect to Google's home page. Google missed a few though. *Googl.com*, *gpogle.com* and *goolgle.com* redirect to sites totally unrelated to Google and would appear to exist simply to profit from the Google brand.

Misspellings can also be incorporated into the content of pages. I recently noticed that a lot of searches to a site I manage used a common misspelling. This occurred in a couple of places in the text and because it was a proprietary term it was not found by the spell checker built into some search engines. I was about to fix the page when I decided to check out the Wordtracker and Overture databases to see how many people searched on the correct and incorrect spelling. I was surprised to find that the misspelling was actually more popular. Checking Google and Yahoo! it was clear that most websites spelt the term correctly so my page had risen to number one in the search results because it was well optimized and there was very little competition.

Common Misspellings

It is fairly easy to come up with misspellings for your target keywords. Try reversing letter combinations, missing letters or using letters close to each other on the keyboard. As an example the letters R and T may get substituted. Phonetic spellings are also common as Ms Spears demonstrates. Before creating pages full of misspellings you should check out whether anyone uses the terms, Overture and Wordtracker are your friends. See how much competition there is from orthographically challenged webmasters. Wikipedia and the Cornell library, amongst other resources, have data on frequently misspelled words:

```
http://en.wikipedia.org/wiki/List_of_common_misspellings
```

```
http://www.library.cornell.edu/tsmanual/TSSU/comis1.html
```

Forums are also a source of common misspellings for specialized areas. For example in skiing many Anglophones spell the French resort *Courchevel* as *Courcheval.*

Incorporating misspellings into web pages is more challenging. Having a site full of spelling mistakes won't impress visitors and potential advertisers much. It would be possible to use techniques such as entry pages which send the user to the correct version of the page. Search engines may see this as a Black Hat technique although if the content of the real and entry pages are identical it is really providing a service to the end user. If your website is database driven you could take a list a common misspellings, words such as *effect* spelt as *affect*, and automatically generate duplicate content pages substituting misspellings for the real words. With the introduction of spell checking of queries by search engines the effects will be somewhat diluted. Google for one also seems to be aware of common misspellings and language differences (e.g. color and colour) and indexes pages with alternate versions of words.

You could also use inbound-links with misspellings in the anchor text. Given the value of good inbound-links this technique should be used sparsely although some kind of internal, search engine friendly, site map with major misspellings could be an idea.

Automatic Correction of URLs

Not directly related to search engine optimization are users that mistype Uniform Resource Locators (URLs), either directly into the browser address bar or webmasters who make errors with links. A typo will generate an error on the web server commonly known as a *404 Not Found* error after its HTTP (HyperText Transfer Protocol) code. It is a good idea to trap these errors and redirect the user either to the home page or to a site map so they can try to find the right link. As part of this process it is also possible to spell check the URL to try and locate the correct resource name. Filters such as *mod_speling* for Apache and *URLSpellCheck* for Microsoft's IIS can provide a simple: *did you mean X?* type of correction.

Microsoft Network (MSN) Search

MSN Search results were based on the Yahoo! Inktomi index. However Microsoft has declared its intention to compete seriously with both Google and Yahoo! in the area of search. If past battles with Digital Research, Lotus, Novell, WordPerfect and Netscape are anything to go by things are going to get very rough and nasty. Microsoft has been caught napping over the rise of Content Targeted Advertising which has done much to revitalize the *dot.com* sector over the last couple of years. The on-line advertising market is now worth more than cinema advertising.

Microsoft's first line of attack is a near dominance in browser technology with Internet Explorer although alternatives such as Opera, Mozilla Firefox and Apple's Safari are making inroads into this market by offering more advanced features such as tabbed browsing and improved security. Currently if a user mistypes a website name Internet Explorer redirects them to the MSN Search engine and this feature must account for a lot of MSN traffic. With control over 90% of user desktops there is no technical reason why Microsoft can't make life very difficult for Google and Yahoo! although a series of lawsuits, albeit with largely toothless judgments, may have tempered Microsoft's use of such practices. Instead Microsoft has thrown down the gauntlet by saying that its new algorithmic search engine will return better results than Google.

Microsoft intends to integrate search into the computer desktop with a user seeing no difference between searching his computer and searching other resources such as the Web. The new search engine will be the backbone of this technology. It underwent Beta trials in 2004 before a full launch in January, 2005. The interface is clean, almost Googlesque and the results also have a Google feel to them, at least in terms of appearance. The relevance of results is currently not perfect and the separation between sponsored and real results is not always obvious. Early users noticed a preference for pages created with Microsoft technology. In theory the search and software arms of Microsoft are separate so this may simply reflect the initial algorithms that were probably tested on Microsoft technology. Still it would be an interesting way to extend the Microsoft hegemony.

Despite being described as an algorithmic search engine the results still seem to currently be influenced by on-page factors and prone to some Black Hat techniques. It is perhaps unfair to criticize the engine this early even though Microsoft has made a lot of noise about this engine. As everyone knows Microsoft rarely gets it right with the initial versions of their products but with deep pockets they are probably in this for the long haul.

Rumors about desktop search, the ability to seamlessly search both the Internet and documents on the local disks, were fueled when Microsoft acquired Lookout Software in June 2004. Lookout has developed a program for searching Outlook email messages. However Microsoft was wrong-footed by the release of Google's desktop search in October 2004. Microsoft had originally announced that this feature would be incorporated into its Longhorn release of the Windows operating system sometime in 2006 with a browser based version being made available "*sometime beforehand*". With the pressure from Google, Microsoft launched their desktop search tool in a browser based version in December, 2004. Yahoo! followed shortly afterwards although their version is not integrated with the browser. Apple is incorporating similar features in their next release of the Macintosh operating system - codenamed Tiger.

The new Microsoft search claims to have around 5 billion pages indexed. They run a blog at:

```
http://blogs.msdn.com/msnsearch/
```

this gives some interesting tidbits about the ongoing development of this engine. There is a URL for submitting websites, currently at:

```
http://search.msn.com/docs/submit.aspx
```

Although the search engine spider is very active and has no trouble picking up sites provided there is an inbound-link from a site already in the index.

Optimizing for MSN Search

With the old MSN search optimizing for Yahoo! meant optimizing for MSN Search as they shared the same Inktomi index. Microsoft doesn't want to give too much away about their algorithmic search engine but the firm has recently been busy on the patent front and there is almost certainly some technology equivalent to Google's Hilltop algorithm that forms the basis of results. According to their blog they also automatically filter pages for search engine spam:

"*The reason that your site is not in our index is that we are detecting the page as spam when we analyze the page to build our index. How can you make sure that this does not happen? The best thing to do is to not spam us. In case you have not read it here is a quick refresher: dirty JavaScript redirects, stuffing alt text, white on white links, off topic links etc. We take this stuff very seriously and we are continuously working to improve our spam detection."*

Of course, detecting the difference between say, white on white text with a black background, which will be visible to an end user and true Black Hat techniques, is difficult and it may be that the MSN search filters are fairly wide in scope. It is probably wise to avoid techniques that could be mistaken for be spam.

MSN Search gives some general tips for optimizing for their engine. The advice has a few red herrings. They list the following items in order of importance:

- The number and quality of sites that link to your pages.

- Keywords and content. Analyze common phrases used by searchers and include them in the copy. Pages should be at least 200 words long.

- Title tag. It should be less than 80 characters long and should make a searcher want to click on the link.

- Description and Keywords Meta tags. The current MSN search doesn't rank on these but the new Beta engine did show some preference for Meta text. This may not continue to the full release.

- Image alt tags. Will Spencer, who maintains the alt.internet.search-engines FAQ, has tested this element and says it is not used by any of the major search engines except when it is enclosed in an anchor element.

- Limit all pages to a reasonable size. MSN Search recommend that an HTML page with no pictures should be under 150 KB.

and they list the following as being search engine unfriendly due to the difficulty search engine robots have with this type of content

- Frames

- Flash

- JavaScript navigation

- HTML Image Maps

- Dynamic URLs

MSN Search supports the Meta Description tag format for adding descriptive text in SERPS but this is not used as part of the site ranking algorithm. If this tag is not present descriptive text is extracted from the page.

N

Newsfeeds

You may have noticed small orange *rss* or *xml* newsfeed icons on some websites you visit. If you click on these you see a collection of article abstracts in XML format (e**X**tensible **M**arkup **L**anguage). Some websites syndicate part of their content via a newsfeed. There are currently two main standards: RSS (Really Simple Syndication) and Atom. Websites can integrate these headlines into their content and software news aggregators enable end users to scan headlines and article summaries and then click on a link to read the article from the site. The Mozilla Thunderbird email client recently added newsfeed aggregator features and Yahoo! allows its users to build custom news pages.

News syndication is a great way to build awareness of your content and drive click-through traffic to your site. This can be done with relative ease and without major expense or ongoing work. Websites that integrate your feed also provide valuable inbound-links with relevant anchor text. Your syndicated content can help build relationships with users who will also look at other content. There are a number of newsfeed directories, including MyYahoo! that can help publicize your syndicated content and also provide inbound-links.

Many Content Management Systems, especially blogging software, offer newsfeeds as part of the package so beyond publicizing your content there may be no further work to do. You may also start a weblog, for example with Google's popular *blogger.com* site, as an adjunct to your main site. Blogger integrates Atom format newsfeeds as standard. The feed must be enabled under the site preferences and can be found in the file *atom.xml* in the home directory.

Software tools such as Tristana Writer:

```
http://www.charlwood.com/tristana/writer/
```

automatically scan existing content, for example a static *what's new* page and then build RSS and Atom syndication files. These can be published using FTP (File Transfer Protocol) to your website.

Once the feed, effectively a URL pointing to a resource on your web server, is running it should be checked with a validator to make sure there are no errors.

The Feed Validator website:

verifies both Atom and RSS feeds. The feed can then be submitted to feed directories, here is a short list:

- http://www.postami.com/
- http://www.terrar.com/
- http://www.fastbuzz.com/
- http://www.completerss.com/
- http://www.blogdigger.com/
- http://www.daypop.com/
- http://www.news-feeds.org/
- http://www.syndic8.com/
- http://www.easyrss.com/
- http://www.feedster.com/
- http://www.2rss.com/

2rss <http://www.2rss.com/> has tools for converting Atom feeds to RSS format and for generating WAP content suitable for cell phones. The sites listed above help end users and site builders find relevant feeds and are also indexed by search engines so providing additional inbound-links to your website.

MyYahoo!

Yahoo! is building a directory of newsfeeds. You can get your site added to this directory by signing up for a MyYahoo! account and then adding your feed to your own MyYahoo! account. The robot that updates MyYahoo is called:

```
YahooFeedSeeker/1.0
```

You can check that Yahoo! is indexing your site by examining your log files:

```
/index.xml HTTP/1.0" 200 5782 "-" "YahooFeedSeeker/1.0
(compatible; Mozilla 4.0; MSIE 5.5;
http://my.yahoo.com/s/publishers.html; users 7; views 368)"
```

This also shows how many people are subscribing to your feed. The Yahoo! agent categorizes and periodically checks feeds. The agent adjusts the frequency of these checks by starting once per hour and then increasing or decreasing the frequency depending on the number of updates. MyYahoo! maintains a cache of results which avoids overwhelming your website.

You can tell MyYahoo! that a feed has been updated by using a special *ping* URL:

```
http://api.my.yahoo.com/rss/ping?<my feed url>
```

To help readers add your site to their MyYahoo! account you can place a link on your home page:

```
<a href="http://add.my.yahoo.com/rss?url=[your RSS URL
here]"><img border=0
src="http://us.il.yimg.com/us.yimg.com/i/us/my/addtomyyahoo.gif"
></a>
```

A side effect of this, but a very important one, is that your site will also get added immediately to the Yahoo! search directory.

News Search

Some search engines offer specialized news search facilities. If your site or news feed has some wider relevance you may be able to get included. Standards are tougher than for feed directories and blog listings. To get included in Google news send an email to:

```
source-suggestions@google.com
```

You can submit your site to Yahoo! news through this page:

```
http://add.yahoo.com/fast/help/us/news/cgi_feedback/
```

RocketNews search over 10,000 Internet sites as well as content sources for current news and information. This is used on their News portal and XML feeds and is resold in a bespoke format to business customers. Newsfeeds can be submitted to RocketNews by sending an email to:

```
newsites@rocketinfo.com
```

When asking to be included give the name of the news source, its URL and the URL for the RSS or Atom if available.

If your site is selected for inclusion this can take anything from 48 hours to a couple of weeks.

Integrating Third-Party Newsfeeds

You can also integrate other people's newsfeeds into your website. Done judiciously this can create highly themed and fresh content, something many search engine algorithms like. The possible downside is that creating outbound-links can dilute the PageRank available for internal pages and presents exit points for site visitors. The content may also be treated as duplicate pages. It is really up to you to experiment and then perform traffic-analysis on your log files and check search results. Robots such as the Googlebot should start to visit your newsfeed pages more frequently due to the changing content. That means that any static content you add will also get indexed. This can be very useful for press releases and product reviews etc.

To integrate a newsfeed you will need a server or web hosting package that supports scripting. JavaScript aggregation will not work because it requires the client, in this case the robot, to run the script in order to see the stories and links. Three good packages for newsfeed aggregation are CaRP:

```
http://www.geckotribe.com/rss/
```

this uses the PHP language, MagpieRSS

```
http://magpierss.sourceforge.net/
```

also written in PHP which can parse Atom as well as RSS newsfeeds and Kattanweb's kwRSS

```
http://www.kattanweb.com/webdev/projects/index.asp?ID=7
```

using Microsoft's ASP. All three have free versions.

Finding Feeds

FaganFinder have a directory of blogs and RSS feeds

```
http://www.faganfinder.com/blogs/
```

O

Off-Page Factors

Due to the ease with which on-page factors can be manipulated search engines now place more weight on so called off-page factors. Google made this form of ranking famous with its patented PageRank algorithm but researchers discussed using ideas such as link anchor text as far back as 1994. Off-page criteria are obtained from sources other than the website.

Inbound Links

Probably the most important of these criteria are the quantity of inbound-links using anchor text containing your target keywords. These should come from pages covering similar topics, preferably from large, long established authority sites. In the case of Google, the higher the PageRank, the better. All other things being equal, a link from a PR6 site is worth around eight to ten times that of a PR5 site. Remember that Google uses all inbound-links in its ranking process, not just those shown by the *backlinks* option of the Google toolbar. If the page has the luxury of many inbound-links then mixing target keywords to cover different queries is a good idea. Since Yahoo! acquired Overture and dumped the Google index it has published an index called Web Rank. This is based on the number of incoming links to a site. It would seem likely that this is also a factor in their ranking process.

Click Density

Some search engines also rank sites based on usage information. This is called Click Density and was pioneered by the DirectHit engine. The search engine monitors the results pages to see which links users actually follow. This is a kind of quality control and is affected by on-page factors such as the Description META tag and other summary information the search engine uses to describe the page.

On-Page Factors

On-Page factors are related directly to the content and structure of the website. This normally consists of pages written in the HyperText Markup Language

(HTML) but also applies to other document formats that are indexed by search engines, for example Microsoft Word or PDF formats. On-page optimization concerns modifying keyword frequency in the URL, Title, Headings, Hypertext Links and Body text. It may also involve reducing redundant HTML code (aka cruft) produced by web page authoring tools and restructuring the site to create better linked and focused page content.

Many search engines now discount the weight given to on-page factors because they give too much scope for abuse by SEO experts. In theory the visible parts of a web page are less prone to manipulation as they have to make sense to readers. However doorway pages with redirections and clever use of style sheets enable different content to be served to search engines and end users.

Each page should target between two and four keywords directly related to the contents. If you feel the need for more keywords then consider splitting your content into separate pages. The Uniform Resource Locator (URL) should contain keywords, separated by hyphens without being too long, around 128 characters is probably a sensible upper limit for the entire URL. The Title tag should contain the keywords with no stop words but arranged to make sense.

```
<TITLE>On Page Optimization</TITLE>
```

This should be the first tag in the Head section of the page. There is evidence that search engines give more weight to factors higher up the page. The content should be properly structured with the use of Heading (H1, H2, H3 etc) tags containing relevant keywords. Search-engines will only index a limited amount of text in HTML tags and using too many keywords will dilute the focus. Don't spam any of these tags, this won't be effective and could result in a penalty.

Keyword and Description Tags

Many website designers spend a lot of time creating Keyword and Description Meta tags. Although these may be read by search engines, for example the description tag is used by Yahoo! to provide a short description of the site in the Search Engine Results Pages, they are not used for ranking pages.

```
<META NAME="description" content="Optimizing On-Page Factors for
Search Engine">
```

Personally I don't bother with them as they bulk out pages for little real benefit. Both Google, Yahoo! and MSN Search will use the text they find on the page as a description so make sure your first header and sentence describe the contents. However some search engine watchers say that the new Microsoft search engine, currently in beta test, puts some weight on meta-tags. There is also evidence to suggest that search engines give more prominence to keywords earlier in the page and some engines will only index a limited amount of body text so making the first paragraph punchy is a good idea.

Image alternate-text tags (ALT tags) are only indexed where the image is part of a hyperlink. However ALT tags are useful for non-graphical browsing and should be employed correctly.

```
<IMG ALT="Description of Image" SRC="image.jpg">
```

Comments are not indexed. Use bold/strong/italic attributes where appropriate.

Write natural copy aimed at the end user and not search engines. Don't worry too much about keyword density for the contents but take the opportunity to include keywords combined in different phrases and orders and create anchor text to related internal pages. Keep the number of links to fewer than 50, and probably less and do not repeat identical link text. Theme related pages should be at the same level in the hierarchy and be linked through the site's menu structure and site map. At least one page at the same level should link back to the home page so that search engines that have traversed a deep-link can index the rest of the website.

Non-HTML formats

For any other document format, e.g. PowerPoint, Adobe PDF etc make sure you at least have a descriptive document title. Try to avoid formats that search engines find hard to understand; even where a search engine can index the file it will carry less information than plain old HTML. Avoid using images to replace text, except occasionally in hyperlinks. Avoid formats such as Flash, Shockwave and animated sitemaps where there is no alternative text. Do not use HTML Frames which some search engines find hard to navigate, use Style Sheets (CSS) instead. Style Sheets should also be used to reduce the amount of formatting within documents. Keep pages to less than 100 kilobytes and preferably not much more than a screen full of text. Where JavaScript or Flash menus are used include plain-text links at the bottom of the page. These will ensure that search engines index the rest of your website.

Other factors directly under the control of the website are the amount of content. Large websites generally rank better than small websites for a number of reasons. Search engines also like fresh content and will spider this more frequently. A regularly updated news page, even a blog, can provide deep links to the rest of the website.

Outbound Links

An outbound-link (OBL) is a link from your website to another website. Outbound links can add value to your site by providing useful information to users without you having to create the content. It is difficult for a single website to be comprehensive about a subject area. At the same time outbound links are a potential jumping off point for users and also provide PageRank for the target page. Some search engines algorithms actually place value on sites with many outbound links. These are dubbed *authority* or *expert sites*.

Be careful about linking to bad neighborhoods, including LinkFarms and heavily optimized sites. These may get your site penalized. Be wary about any site with zero PageRank or that can't be found in search engines. Check that it has not been banned for some reason. A single link to a *bad neighborhood* is unlikely to cause problems but combined with other factors it could be viewed in a poor light by search engines.

It is possible to open outbound links in a new browser window using the HTML target="_new" operator:

```
<a href="" target="_new">
```

but many users and web designers don't like this as it breaks the natural back and forward navigation provided by the browser.

P

Page Jacking

Anyone who runs a content rich website will be familiar with other sites ripping off their content. Sometimes this is done with an outbound-link back to the original content, sometimes it is more blatant and sometimes it is even an error. I've had content copied by companies and organizations that should really know better. Many people forget that just because something is on the Web it is still subject to copyright laws. Unfortunately with the Web being such an international medium enforcing those laws can be difficult. It is an unfortunate situation, the Web was designed to allow easy linking to useful content but it seems too tempting for some people just to copy and paste what they find to enhance their own website.

Wholesale rip-offs of multiple pages, even whole sites, happen. This is referred to as page-jacking. The jacked pages are identical to the originals, same titles, Meta-data and content. There are two motivations for page jacking, more themed content can increase the overall ranking of a site to search engines and the stolen pages can earn money through product sales or via Content Targeted Advertising. The danger for the original site is that Black Hat SEOers can boost the stolen pages far above their own in search engine results and duplicate content algorithms may actually penalize the original website.

Redirects

A more technically complex form of jacking sucks the content directly off your website by screen scraping. Recently site owners have seen an even more advanced technique using page redirects. When Googlebot and AltaVista's Scooter see temporary a '302' redirect sent by the web server or a Meta refresh tag contained in an HTML page they index the redirected content but keep the URL of the page making the redirect.

```
<meta http-equiv="refresh" content="0; url=http://www.original-
site.com/">
```

If the site uses cloaking techniques it can serve these redirects just to search engine robots and serve other pages to visitors. The effect is twofold, the original site vanishes from search engine results pages and the new site picks up the ranking of the original. This can be used to feed traffic through to other pages in the site. This tactic is becoming more common and hopefully search engines will address it in the near future. It can also occur accidentally as some web directories use redirects to link to sites so they can count click-throughs.

If you notice a large drop in traffic from a particular search engine it is worth investigating whether your site has been a victim of page-jacking. Copyscape:

```
http://www.copyscape.com/
```

can take a URL to one of your web pages and search for copies or part copies. You can do the same by taking unique phrases and typing them into search engines. A redirect page will contain your description and title but will have the URL of the page-jacker's website. If you click on the *cache* link on Google or Yahoo! you will see what the robot actually indexed, which will be your original page.

If the copying is unintentional then an email to the webmaster will usually be sufficient to get the content removed. This won't work with more hardcore page-jackers. Use a tool such as *whois* or *SamSpade*:

```
http://www.samspade.org
```

to discover who claims to own the site and who is their Internet Service Provider or Web Hosting company. Find out if they are selling products through an affiliate scheme or using content target advertising. Contact all these people pointing out the problem, you can do this by email in the first instance but follow up with a fax is there is no quick response. In the case of Redirects the websites are not actually copying your content, just exploiting the way search engines sometimes index pages. Search engines and ISPs are notoriously unresponsive so you should fax as well as email. You can quote the Digital Millennium Copyright Act which might elucidate a quicker response.

```
http://www.google.com/dmca.html
```

Technical solutions to redirects by the website are not possible as the problem is with the search engine robot. There will be no referrer information and the visit will look just like a normal visit by the robot. The search engine could block sites with large numbers of *302 redirects* although there are genuine reasons for their use.

Digital Millennium Copyright Act and Search Engines

The Digital Millennium Copyright Act (DCMA) was introduced by the United States to comply with World Trade Organization treaties covering intellectual property. The DCMA affords search engines and ISPs some protection if they are found to be inadvertently hosting or indexing material that infringes someone's copyright. However to benefit from that protection they must remove the material or reference if notified of the fact by the copyright holder. Search engines have different procedures for enforcing copyright infringements.

Cyber Rights

The Electronic Frontier Foundation (EFF) maintains a website on online rights which may be useful when looking for assistance after a copyright infringement:

```
http://www.chillingeffects.org/
```

PageRank

PageRank is the concept that enabled Google to leap-frog over other search engines during the late 1990s in terms of relevant search engine results pages and speed of search. PageRank holds US patent number 6,285,999 granted on the 4th September 2001 to Larry Page, one of Google's founders. Page's idea is based on established practice for scientific papers where the importance of a paper is based on the number of citations made to it by other papers. The Google algorithm interprets a link from one page to another as a vote. The Google algorithm and the configuration of web pages means that PageRank can be fed back so that pages that have more votes are then deemed to be more important and the votes they cast (outbound-links) are subsequently given more weight.

Many web designers' efforts to optimize their sites for search engines, if they make any efforts at all, stop at acquiring inbound-links and exchanging links with other websites in the hope that this will boost their site's PageRank. This focus on PageRank is probably due in part to the Google toolbar that can be installed on Microsoft's Internet Explorer web browser. This shows a PageRank value for the current site on a scale of 0 to 10.

Getting a good site ranking is not quite as simple as getting a good score on the Google toolbar and decisions about outbound-links and site structure can have significant effects on PageRank.

Fortunately because of the patent the theory behind PageRank is known. The formula is relatively simple:

$$\text{Page Rank} = (1 - \partial) + \partial \times \sum_{i=1}^{n} \frac{PR^n}{C^n}$$

Where

∂	damping factor, given as 0.85
n	total number of inbound links
PRn	page rank of inbound page n
Cn	number of outbound links from page n

So the PageRank (PR) for any page is equal to some constant value (0.15) plus the sum of all the page ranks from inbound links divided by the number of links (C) on each corresponding page multiplied by the damping factor (0.85).

Don't worry if that is too hard to visualize, we will look at some real examples below. One more thing before we do. As pages can, and usually do, feedback to other pages by way of hyperlinks the calculation has to be made iteratively. Every time Google visits a page it recalculates the PageRank based on the weights of the inbound links. Assuming no other changes it takes around 40 iterations for the figure to converge to a stable value although Google itself uses linear algebra to reduce the number of calculations. The damping factor (∂) is set at 0.85 for optimum performance.

A Page with no Inbound Links

```
Page Rank = 1 - 0.85 = 0.15
```

Theoretically a page with no inbound links has a page rank of 0.15. However such a page could only be found by the Google robots if it was added to the index by the Google submission page. Creating such orphan pages is not a good idea as they cannot be found by users but what it does imply is that pages within a site can gain PageRank by creating pages and by linking those pages internally. Ideally such a site should have at least one inbound link from another site in the Google index. Google therefore favors large, well linked sites.

Inbound Link from a Page with many Outbound Links

The second part of equation, PR / C, is also very interesting. This means that each page that links to us increases our PageRank in proportion to its own value. The higher the PageRank the greater the increase. However the PageRank is split over all the outbound links on the page. So if a single inbound link comes from a page with a rank of 6 with 6 other outbound links on that page the increase to us is:

```
Page Rank = (1 - 0.85) + 0.85 x (6.0 / 6.0) = 1.0
```

Whereas if there was only a single outbound link to our page, the increase would be 5.25.

Calculating Page Ranks

It takes quite a bit of work to calculate stable PageRank figures even for simple examples. Rather than do this by hand there are tools on the Web that show the effects of simple site structures with inbound and outbound links. We have used Paul Ryan's page rank calculator which you can find at

```
http://webworkshop.net/pagerank_calculator.php3
```

It is very illustrative and the following simple examples will give you a feel for what happens with different linking scenarios.

Before we go further another interesting feature of the PageRank calculation is that the average of all the PageRanks in a closed system is 1.0. The entire

Google index is just such a system. If you took all the pages in the index, added the page ranks together then divided this by the total number of pages the result would be 1.0. This means that there is a finite amount of PageRank to share out, as people add pages and these get indexed, the PageRank of existing pages decreases.

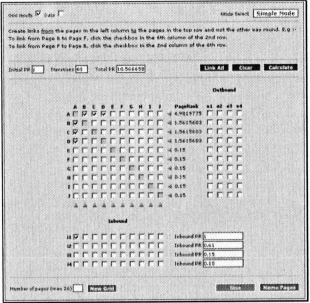

Figure 9. PageRank Calculator for a hierarchy with one inbound link

This has a major implication: Content poor, small, badly linked sites are less interesting than large, content rich sites. We are, of course, defining content purely in terms of the number of pages in a site.

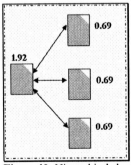

Figure 10. Hierarchical closed site

To illustrate this point look at the site in figure 10. It is a closed set of pages, essentially no different from the whole Google universe. Remember from the example above that an orphan page has an intrinsic page rank of 0.15. But what have we here? The page rank of the home page is 1.92 and the other sub-pages 0.69. How did that happen? Well the PageRank of the home page is equal to:

```
(1 - 0.15) + 0.85 x ((0.15/1) + (0.15/1) + (0.15/1)) = 0.5325
```

We feed this figure into the sub-pages to get their PageRank:

```
(1 - 0.15) + 0.85 x (0.5325/3) = 0.300875
```

We then feed this figure back to the homepage. The PageRank calculator given above can show you all the intermediate calculations. The figures pretty much reach their final values after 18 iterations. If you add all the page ranks together and divide by the total number of pages, four, the result is 1.0. We have a fixed size pot which is distributed amongst the pages by the linking structure.

Hierarchical Structures

Figure 10 is an example of a hierarchy. These are fairly common in the real world and are therefore often used on websites, for example to represent a company and its divisions etc. If each page links back to the top of the hierarchy the effect is to concentrate PageRank in this entry page. All other factors being equal a higher PageRank will mean that this page appears first in the search results. As this is the main entry point to the hierarchy this is a good thing. Adding more levels to the hierarchy will further boost the PageRank of the entry page.

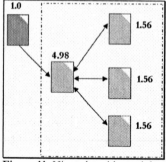

Figure 11. Hierarchy with one inbound-link

The effect of a single inbound link from a page with a PageRank of 1.0 is even more striking. This page must itself have some inbound links to have this PageRank and these are not shown in this diagram. The addition of this link has more than doubled all the PageRanks of our site because of the internal feedback effect.

Interlinked Structures

Sometimes we have more interlinking between pages. An online presentation would have back and forward buttons to enable navigation between individual slides. Some authoring tools (Microsoft FrontPage springs to mind) can automatically create links between all pages within the same level of a hierarchy as shown in figure 12.

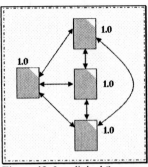

Figure 12. Interlinked Structure

More interlinking has the effect of spreading PageRank about the website. In the case of figure 12, where every page links to every other page, the PageRank is 1.0.

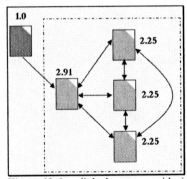

Figure 13. Interlinked structure with single inbound-link

Figure 13 shows an interlinked or mesh structure with a single inbound link. Again the boost to our internal pages is more than doubled but this is distributed more evenly. Our home page still gets the lion's share of the increase because it is directly linked with the external page.

So we can use our link structure to distribute PageRank from inbound links around our site. How we distribute that PageRank is directly under our control. At the same time we want to leave a logical navigation structure for users of our website.

Adding Pages

Each page that is added to a site increases the total amount of PageRank available for distribution in the site by 1.0 but because there are more pages the average PageRank remains at 1.0, assuming no inbound links. If we add thousands of pages all linking back to the home page with little interlinking, we can significantly boost the PageRank of this page. An effect that has been noticed by Black Hat SEO experts.

To increase the average PageRank of our site we need to get inbound links. As the Google universe is in equilibrium with an average PageRank of 1.0, for every site with an above average PageRank there must be other sites with below average PageRank. This brings us nicely onto PageRank leakage.

Outbound Links and PageRank Leakage

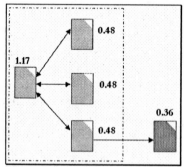

Figure 14. Effect of an outbound-link

In theory an outbound link doesn't directly affect the PageRank of the page containing the outbound link. The calculation is applied to the target page. What it does do is dilute some of the PageRank from the source page that would otherwise be fed back into the system. That is the 'C' (number of outbound-links) part of the equation we looked at earlier. We've seen that feedback is a powerful multiplier of PageRank.

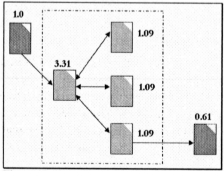

Figure 15. Site with one inbound-link and one outbound-link

If we take our original closed hierarchy and add a single outbound link we immediately see a big difference. The sub-page now divides the vote it used to send exclusively back to the homepage with another external page. This means less boost for the home page and therefore less PageRank transferred to the other sub-pages. The overall PageRank for the site has dropped from 4.0 to 2.61. That's more than a page of content. The site is leaking PageRank to the outside world. This is why a few sites, such as Microsoft.com are PageRank titans while thousands of other sites are PageRank minnows. Your outbound link increases the chances that someone will follow that link to another site, PageRank reflects that possibility.

Figure 15 shows the effect of a site with one outbound and one inbound-link. Again the effect is to transfer PageRank we acquired from our inbound-link to another site.

How I Learned to Stop Worrying and Love PageRank

This should give you a pretty thorough grounding in PageRank theory. PageRank is a patented process used by Google. Although Google is a very important search engine for optimization it is worth remembering that PageRank is just one of over a hundred factors that control its results. We've also discussed the algorithm described in the original patent. Google has made many tweaks to their algorithms over the years and this may include the PageRank process. PageRank is certainly less important than it was and algorithms such as Hilltop and Local Rank may actually favor the creation of expert or authority pages with many outbound-links. There are two important positive side effects to good PageRank, it creates inbound-links which can feed click through traffic from other sites and if good anchor text is used this will be a plus point with all the major search engines. In addition it encourages good site structure and linking practices.

In all the examples we have quoted PageRanks as decimals whereas the Google toolbar shows them as whole numbers. In fact the real calculated PageRank figures range from 0.15 to some very, very high values. The Yahoo homepage probably has a PageRank of billions. How these get mapped onto the 0-10 scale is discussed further in the Google Toolbar section. Just be aware that the toolbar value gives a very simplified view of what is really happening with PageRank.

Site structure plays a significant role in distributing the PageRank available to a site. Use hierarchies with links back to important entry pages to concentrate page rank on those pages. These pages should target your most competitive choice of keywords. All pages can link back to the homepage. Create as much content as possible, long pages can be split into smaller chunks and these may be interlinked to distribute their PageRank evenly.

Outbound-Links and Link Hoarding

Don't worry too much about PageRank leakage (some SEO'ers prefer the term dilution as it isn't really a leak). The examples given above are very simple. We'll discuss some techniques for mitigating PageRank dilution under the site map and cross-linking sections. Link hoarding is also badly viewed by other websites that may provide inbound-links. You will inevitably link to worthwhile, external sites just as other sites will link to you. Think of PageRank as money, use it and spend it wisely but remember there is more to good SEO than PageRank alone.

Queries

Knowledge about how search engines work and they are actually used is very useful to search engine optimizers. Google heralded the era of lazy searching, or search for the masses, depending on your point of view. Before Google, using the top dog, AltaVista required an arcane knowledge of Boolean logic and obscure syntax to get the most out of the engine. With Google, and increasingly with rivals such as Yahoo! and MSN's so called *algorithmic search*, you simply have to type your query and normally you find what you are looking for in the first few results. The relevancy is so good that the majority of searchers don't look beyond the first results page.

A survey by OneStat that examines search engine use has shown that searchers are becoming more sophisticated with an increase in the use of two and three search terms in queries. The implication for page optimization is that more specialized pages targeting niche terms are the immediate future. Some searchers are surprised to type in a query:

```
kw1 kw2
```

and find pages where the keywords do not actually appear on the page. This is because off-page optimizations such as anchor text have been taken into account by the search engine algorithm. On Google you can use the *intext* operators to restrict the search to page contents. In terms of Boolean logic the above search includes all the terms, in any order and is the equivalent of

```
kw1 AND kw2
```

If you want to find any of the words you can use *OR* instead of *AND*. Some search engines will exclude common words. These can be included by putting a '+' operator in front of the keyword:

```
kw1 +kw2
```

Conversely the '-' operator can be used to exclude keywords

An exact phrase can be matched by putting the words in quotes:

```
"to be or not to be"
```

Stop words will still be excluded from the search. You can mix and match

```
"to be or not to be" Jack Benny
```

the asterisk '*' character is used as a wildcard, it will match any word:

```
"to be * to be"
```

Matching exact terms can be useful for search engine optimizers who want to see if a new page that has recently been spidered by the search engine robot can be found in the index. Initially these pages may rank too low to be found using target keywords but may be found by entering a phrase from the page content.

General search queries often return far too many results. With a pool of some billions of pages to choose from it doesn't really matter if the results are comprehensive so long as some relevant links are included on the first page of results. To cope with information overload when searching for specific information go detailed first then zoom out and favor obscure keywords in the search.

There are some handy operators that can be used to analyze site rankings in search engine results pages. The *site:* operator restricts the search to a specific website:

```
site:www.seochat.com serps
```

If you just enter the site restriction with no keywords you get an idea of how many pages from your website are indexed by that search engine:

```
site:www.seochat.com
```

```
(Google: 23,300, MSN Search 2,323 and Yahoo! 1)
```

Clearly there is some problem with seochat.com at Yahoo!

You can restrict your search to top level domains:

```
search engine optimization site:edu
```

This search will only find pages from educational establishments. Or you could search just in a particular country:

```
axis of weasel site:fr
```

When I tried this the first page returned was from the French President's website!

The link operator shows the number of inbound-links (backlinks) for a site:

```
link:http://www.seochat.com
```

```
(Google: 57,000, MSN Search 56,277 and Yahoo! 536,000)
```

The figure for the new MSN search is maybe not surprising but why is the value for Google so low compared to Yahoo! Google doesn't show low PageRanked inbound-links. This makes some sense for them as their PageRank algorithm will place much less importance on such links. In addition the Google toolbar often doesn't give the exact ranking for sites, making analysis of Google's algorithms more difficult.

The special operators *intitle* and *inurl* work with both Google and Yahoo search and restrict the keyword matching to the web address and page title. This can be useful for understanding which elements of a page are important to the search engine results and can be used to analyze competition.

Search engines are constantly adding new features. For example, Yahoo and Google let you specify file formats.

Sometimes new features have unintended consequences. When Google introduced number range searching the first thing many people thought of was looking for credit card numbers that had inadvertently been indexed by search engines:

```
mastercard 5132000000000000..5231999999999999
```

Google supports date ranges as well. This shows when the page last changed in the Google index. The Google web interface only gives a limited set of options but you can use the *daterange* operator directly:

```
http daterange:2453332-2453333
```

finds all the documents updated between the 23rd and 24th of November 2004, well over a million of them. The date format uses the Julian calendar which is a count of days since January 1, 4713 BC. The Julian calendar doesn't require complicated leap century calculations or those accounting for missing days involved with the changeover from Julian to the Gregorian calendars.

The search engine's own help pages are often wrong or simply out of date. As an example Google claims that the *site:* operator can be used on news stories but this is not supported.

Alternative Query Interfaces

Fagan Finder has an alternative interface to the major search engines giving all the available search options

```
http://www.faganfinder.com/engines.html
```

R

Recycling Domains

A source of inbound-links and high search engine rankings are old domains. This is another technique that was pioneered by the on-line porn industry. It has been estimated that close to a million domain names are not renewed each month. Couple this with dead blogs and there is a lot of potential for recycling other people's optimization efforts. Domains are typically registered for a 2 year period. When a domain (*.com*, *.net* etc) comes up for renewal the registrar sends a renewal notice to the owner. If there is no response then on expiry the domain goes a holding phase that can last up to 45 days. During this time the registrar can send a delete command. There then follows a 30 day Redemption Grace Period (RGP) which gives the owner a last chance to renew the domain. A five day *deletion* delay follows before the name becomes available for registration.

Given that a lot of the best web virtual-estate was registered during the dot.com boom the fact that many website owners are failing to renew domain names has not gone unnoticed. Search engine optimizers will be in competition with people looking for brandable domains for a new wave of e-Commerce ventures. Domain name registrars have caught on to this business and will grab expired, high value domains that they manage with the hope of reselling for inflated prices. There is also a third market in domain names, recently the domain: *mychildren.com* was offered on the auction site eBay.com with a reserve of $100,000. The site had a Google PageRank of zero. The name didn't attract any bids.

There are a number of services that will show domains that are due for renewal. Some of these are associated with registrars and presumably have an inside knowledge of domains that are about to expire, others are more dubious and appear to be selling domains that have not been registered but have been generated by software and then checked against the *whois* database to see if they are available.

You can find expired domain names from directories. Link checker programs such as XenuLink Sleuth:

```
http://home.snafu.de/tilman/xenulink.html
```

can be used to automatically traverse directories looking for broken external links which may indicate an expired domain name. The best bet is to concentrate initially on sites sharing the same theme. Using one section of a large web based directory I was able to find a few candidate domains which were either expired or soon to expire.

From an SEO viewpoint it is only worth considering domains with existing inbound-links, and therefore good Google PageRank. Inbound links are an important ranking factor not just with Google but MSN Search, Yahoo! and other search engines. PageRank, a Google concept, is used simply as a measure of a domain's worth in SEO terms. Once you have a list of target domain names you can use a bulk PageRank checker such as:

```
http://www.top25web.com/pagerank.php
```

to sort the wheat from the chaff. One of the sites I found had a 6/10 PageRank and was currently detagged by the registrar awaiting cancellation.

The question is, what do you do with any domains you pick up? Well you can repoint them directly to your website. This is what *fashionmall.com* did when it acquired the ill-stared *boo.com* domain name for £250,000. Readers may remember that boo.com was the fashion retailer that personified the folly and hubris of the dot.com era by burning $135 million in venture capital in less than 12 months. The problem with this is that it can dilute your online identity, especially with search engines that will see identical content under two different domains.

If the site contents on your recycled domain differ markedly from the original you may lose inbound-links as webmasters notice the change. In addition the site's theme and the anchor text on inbound-links may no longer match which may cause some search engines to discount the site's value. An alternative is to put up a micro-site matching the original contents and then link across to your site(s).

Blogs

Of course registering domain names costs money, although it might still prove to be cheaper and more effective than buying links or directory listings. An alternative it to recover old weblogs (blogs) from free blog sites such as *blogspot.com*. Blogs range from simple online journals to full blown electronic news publications. They cover a range of topics and because they are simple to set up they have drawn in a Diaspora of users with little knowledge of HTML or web publishing. The blog software means that pages are published in search engine friendly and standards complaint HTML using static URLs. Bloggers (as blog writers are called) are very free with linking to other websites and each other so many blogs have acquired good inbound-links. The blogging craze has cooled somewhat of late and there are many blogs around that have not been updated for at least a couple of years. Some bloggers want to simply move on and so delete their blogs and this last category can be optimization gold dust.

You will need to find out what error text the blog gives for a deleted blog, for example *blog not found*. Search for deleted blogs that have a good PageRank. Remember that toolbar PageRank is a logarithmic scale; you might need 10 PR3 blogs to give the same benefit as a single PR4 blog. The SEOChat PageRank Search will show search results and their toolbar PageRank:

```
http://www.seochat.com/seo-tools/pagerank-search/
```

Restrict your search to the blog's domain using the *site* operator.

```
Page not found site:blogsite.com
```

Look down the list for any blogs that don't have any descriptive text in the search results. Not all of these will be deleted and some may already have been reclaimed. Select the highest PR blogs, you definitely don't want to be reclaiming PR0 blogs. Register with the blogsite and recreate the blog. It is likely that some blogging sites will take steps to stop blogs from being reclaimed; such as putting a delay on how quickly dead blogs can be reused.

You will want to optimize the blog template, if possible, to remove extraneous links such as profile information then simply create a post with a link over to your main site. Your post will need a bit of content and don't forget to use keywords in your anchor text.

Creating dummy blogs in this way is most definitely a Black Hat technique. It won't make you popular with the blogsite owners or search engines but with so many blogs being created and abandoned each day it is doubtful that anyone will actually notice. Remember what Google has said that linking to a site cannot do that site harm.

You could actually run your blog as a complimentary news site to your main site. Some blog software provides newsfeeds which can be useful for getting listed in Yahoo! and on news feed aggregators.

eBay Domain Auctions

The online auction site ebay.com runs auctions for domain names, these can be found under:

```
Computers & Networking → Other Hardware & Services → Domain
Names
```

Robots and Spiders

Search engines run programs called robots to automatically traverse a website's link structure retrieving documents. The process of retrieving pages from the website is often called *spidering* or *crawling* and robots are therefore also referred to as spiders or web-crawlers. A search engine will run many such robots simultaneously. The robot finds a website either through a URL submitted directly to the engine by the webmaster, by following a link from another site or by a user visiting the site with one of the search engine toolbars installed on his browser.

The robot may not enter from the site's home page. This implies that every page of the site should be reachable from the entry page. The easiest way to achieve this is to put a link to the home page on each page within the site.

From the point of view of the web server the robot works in much the same way as a browser. It requests a page and downloads the content. Any URLs in the page are extracted and these are added to the list of pages to be indexed. The page is then passed on to an indexer program. This extracts the content of the page including elements such as titles, headings and paragraphs and indexes them in accordance with the search engine's algorithms. Other rules may be applied such as keyword proximity. Search engines are using increasingly sophisticated algorithms which may also consider groups of pages in order to identify themes.

If the page is large the robot may retrieve just the first part and may only follow the first few links. Google currently indexes around 100 kilobytes of a file (text and markup), Yahoo! will index somewhat more. It is possible to conduct an experiment by finding a long file: word lists, glossaries and dictionaries are a good source, then query terms that occur to the bottom of the page. For example the following search in Google:

```
"The Climbing Dictionary" abseil adze filetype:htm
```

Returns a 163 kilobyte glossary of climbing terms, whereas

```
"The Climbing Dictionary" abseil adze portaledge filetype:htm
```

Returns a different web page because the term: *portaledge* occurs around the 110 kilobytes point in the first page and so was not indexed. Interestingly the cache version shows the complete file but claims it is only 101 kilobytes long. Yahoo!, on the other hand, has no trouble with the second query and indexed the complete document. The Googlebot also takes a number of visits in order to follow a large number of outbound-links (50+) on a single page. The bottom line is that web authors should try to keep pages fairly short with the most important content and links towards the top of the page. Dividing content into shorter pages has a number of advantages:

- there is a greater possibility for interlinking content with meaningful anchor text

- less bandwidth is used on the server

- pages can be better focused on target keywords

- Content Targeted Advertising can be more specific and stays visible on the page

Common Problems

An important thing to understand is that a page will not appear in a search engine's index until it has been visited by the search engine's robot. This is where knowledge of log-file traffic analysis is very useful. Most robots identify themselves and can be found by looking at the website's log files. Real web hosting with access to raw logs is essential for SEO. Third party traffic counters will not provide this information as they rely on the web browser downloading an image file or running some JavaScript. Robots don't do this.

```
66.196.90.36 [01/Oct/2004:00:01:04 +0100] "GET /index.htm
HTTP/1.0" 200 6025 "-" "Mozilla/5.0 (compatible; Yahoo! Slurp;
http://help.yahoo.com/help/us/ysearch/slurp)"
```

The robot identifies itself using the User-Agent HTTP header. In this case it is Yahoo's slurp. It fetched the home page: *index.htm* on the 1st of October. Two interesting pieces of information that should be checked are the HTTP response code and the number of bytes sent. These are shown in bold, *200* is OKAY and the size is correct. Also note that there is no referrer information. Robots fetch pages based on their own list compiled by the search engine's indexing program not by following links around the site in real time.

The following table lists some of the most common search engine robots:

User Agent	Search Engine
Scooter	AltaVista
Slurp	Yahoo!, Inktomi, MSN Search, HotBot, Lycos Europe
Googlebot	Google
msnbot	MSN Algorithmic Search
Sidewinder etc.	Infoseek

Table 3. Common search engine robots

Robots have a poor understanding of JavaScript, HTML Frames and multimedia content such as Flash animations. Each request for a page stands on its own. Robots can't manage cookies, session ids and don't provide referrer information. They are unable to access password-protected areas. This has the advantage that extraneous information such as member profiles in forums, effectively noise for a robot, can be hidden from any user not logged in to the site.

There are a number of reasons why a page doesn't appear in the search engine results pages:

- The page is too deep within the site's hierarchy or not correctly linked. Check internal links and consider adding a site map to allow every page to be accessed within two jumps from the home page

- The website was unreachable due to Name Server DNS or routing problems. Internet routing problems can be hard to track down, the page may be accessible from one location but not from the search engine.

- The web server was down. Normally search engines will retry a number of times before giving up or delisting a page. If the web hosting is unreliable the site should be moved elsewhere.

- Dynamic pages are used. Dynamic pages are not in themselves a problem but long query strings and dynamic URLs pose problems for search engine robots.

- The site uses HTML Frames. This is common with domain cloaking.

- The site is protected by a robots.txt file

- The site has been page-jacked, at the time of writing this seems to be a feature in Yahoo's and Google's handling of redirects, the page will get indexed as a result of a redirect from another page, but it is the redirecting page that appears in the results. Googlebot or Slurp will appear in the log-files but the site can't be found in search results.

- The web server has trouble serving content to the robot. Robots typically accept HTML and text pages. They indicate this to the web server by sending the HTTP Header:

```
Accept: text/html and text/plain
```

some badly configured web servers reject this with an HTTP 406 (no acceptable content) error. You can test this with the command line URL (cUrl) utility:

```
curl -H "Accept: text/html" http://mydomain.com/
```

There are web based tools that aim to show you a search engine spider's view of your page:

```
http://searchengineworld.com/cgi-bin/sim_spider.cgi
```

As a rule the simpler the pages the more likely they are to get indexed by search engine robots. This is a case where flashy, corporate sites often lose out.

In order to work out which pages are not getting indexed and why, it is necessary to dig a little deeper. Log file analysis tools can give some general trends but more specific problems may require a more detailed analysis of individual log entries. If your site is reasonably popular searching log files directly can be a daunting business. On a site with 100,000 page views per month the log file may hold close to a million entries.

The first useful piece of information is to see how many pages are indexed by a search engine. The command

```
site:yoursite.com
```

Works with MSN Search, Yahoo! and Google and will return a list of all the indexed pages. For a well structured site that has been around for some time this figure should be similar to the total number of pages on the site, give or take any changes made over the last couple of months such as adding new content.

If there is a big difference, and there often is, take a look through the checklist above. If you are running Linux or Mac OS/X or have the Red Hat Cygwin toolset installed on your Windows PC there are some useful text analysis tools that you can run from a command line window. Windows's users can open the log file into Excel using the space character as a column separator. The only problem is that Excel will not accept more than 32,000 lines.

First of all find all the redirects and error lines for the search engine's robot over at least the previous month. This can be done with *grep* (native Windows versions of this command can be found on the Web):

```
grep " 30.* *googlebot" mydomain.log
grep " 40.* *googlebot" mydomain.log
```

The first command says search for all the lines containing the string " *30*" followed by a single character followed by any number of characters then finally the word *googlebot*. This is grep regular expression syntax and is a very powerful tool for pattern matching for text in files. Further explanation is beyond the scope of this book. *Teach Yourself Regular Expressions in 10 Minutes* by Ben Forta explains the subject in more detail.

Redirects (HTTP 30* errors) are not a problem if the robot subsequently fetches the redirected page. HTTP 40* errors may be due to missing resources or server configuration problems. Search engine robots are very slow at updating their list of URLs to index and may take many months to remove deleted or move pages. This is reasonable as resources are sometimes temporarily unavailable when they come to call.

The following series of commands will extract all the requests by googlebot from the log file, the 7th column is cut from this list and is sorted and any duplicates removed:

```
grep googlebot mydomain.log | cut -d' ' -f7 | sort | uniq
```

The results can be compared with the files on the website to find out which resources are not being indexed by the search engine. Use the checklist to determine the nature of the problem. If the content is recent then the robot may not yet have the resource on its list of pages.

Redirects

There are three ways to redirect a search engine elsewhere, the first two are named after their HTTP response codes and are: *302 Moved Temporarily* and *301 Move Permanently*. It is also possible to use a Meta Refresh tag in the page doing the redirecting:

```
<head>
<meta http-equiv="REFRESH"
content="0;URL=http://newsite.com/index.htm">
</head>
```

A refresh is a two stage process. The robot connects to the page and gets told about the new location. It may then act on this information to access the new page. This second access should be visible at some point in the server log files.

The effects of the *302* and Meta Refresh can be undesirable with both pages being indexed by search engines depending on internal and external inbound-links or one of the pages being dropped due to duplicate page algorithms. In the case of Google the results can vary depending on the exact search term entered. A number of leading companies, *apple.com* and *microsoft.com* included, incorrectly use *302* redirects to merge their domain.com and www.domain.com names as discussed in the Uniform Resource Locator chapter. It seems that the search engines eventually sort it all out, at least in the case of these old and high PageRank sites.

The effect of a *301* redirect is much clearer in the logs. Here the Googlebot first fetches the page *index.html* but gets redirected to *index.htm*

```
crawl-66-249-65-131.googlebot.com - crawl-66-249-65-
131.googlebot.com.5337109924
5954889 [31/Oct/2004:18:05:54 +0000] "GET /index.html HTTP/1.1"
301 242 "-" "Mozilla/5.0 (compatible; Googlebot/2.1;
+http://www.google.com/bot.html)"

crawl-66-249-65-131.googlebot.com - crawl-66-249-65-
131.googlebot.com.5334109924
595576 [31/Oct/2004:18:05:55 +0000] "GET /index.htm HTTP/1.1"
200 4782 "-" "Mozilla/5.0 (compatible; Googlebot/2.1;
+http://www.google.com/bot.html)"
```

It processes this redirect immediately.

As redirects are a two step process they are wasteful of resources and can cause problems as we have discussed. In some cases it is better to use server side aliases to directly serve the new content.

Robot Wrangling

Well behaved robots check whether they are welcome before crawling all over a site. When they first visit they look for a file called *robots.txt* in the home directory. After accessing a page robots may also examine the Meta tags in the header. These give certain ground rules a robot should obey.

```
207.68.146.56 - 207.68.146.56.177651096585556488
[01/Oct/2004:00:05:56 +0100] "GET /robots.txt HTTP/1.0" 200 157
"-" "msnbot/0.3 (+http://search.msn.com/msnbot.
htm)"
```

Robots.txt consists of one or more records separated by blank lines listing the robot's User Agent string and the resources it is not allowed to access:

```
User-agent: msnbot
Disallow: /gates-sucks.htm

User-agent: Slurp
Disallow: /cgi-bin/      # don't index programs
```

Comments begin with a hash '#' character. The wildcard '*' is used to specify all robots. We may wish to exclude the robot from temporary files or administration scripts that we don't want to be found easily. Do not rely on this for security.

If you don't have access to the home directory of your server you can use Robots META tags. Interpretation can differ slightly between robots.

```
<META NAME="ROBOTS" CONTENT="NOINDEX, NOFOLLOW">
```

if you only want to instruct Google's robot replace ROBOT with googlebot. You can use a combination of the following terms:

- noindex: the document will not be included in the search engine's index

- nofollow: the search engine will not follow any links in the page

- noarchive: (some robots only) do not keep a cached copy of the page on the search engine

Google Image Search

Some websites don't like their images being indexed directly by Google. Recently *Perfect 10* magazine went as far as trying to sue Google for copyright infringement on the grounds that Google reproduces a picture of the scantily clad young ladies that feature in Perfect 10 in its results.

Google uses a separate robot for image search; the following entry in robots.txt will keep the image crawler off your site:

```
User-agent: Googlebot-Image
Disallow: /
```

Google's URL Controller

The URL controller:

```
http://services.google.com/urlconsole/controller
```

lets you remove a dead URL (one that results in server *404* error) from Google's index. You will need to register for the service. This can be useful if you move material and the Google robot continues to try to spider the old URL.

Macromedia Flash

The Flash file format has become very popular; it enables web designers to express their creativity. The format has become so pervasive on corporate websites that the phrase *flashturbation* has been coined to describe the design.

Robots have trouble with most documents that are not text or HTML. Some search engines, notably Google, index Word, PowerPoint and PDF documents. To overcome these problems Macromedia have built a utility that can extract text descriptions and hyperlinks from Flash files. The program has been made available to search engines.

Flash and similar formats should still be treated with caution. Indexing will take more resources so a search engine may not do it as a priority, if at all. It will also be harder to optimize such content.

Bad Robots

Not all robots are good. Some roam the Web looking for security holes, probing for known weaknesses in web servers and Content Management Systems. Gateways for sending email are particularly sought after as they can be used by spammers to hide the origins of their junk email. Other robots harvest email addresses from web pages to add to spam lists. Examples are *EmailSiphon* and *Cherry Picker* and they are normally referred to as spambots.

Some robots may appear to be more benign. A site I manage was recently visited by a robot identifying itself as:

```
NPBot
```

it belongs to Name Protect, a company that searches the Web for its clients looking for intellectual property infringements on your server. Nothing much wrong with that except that the robot consumes resources and the results will not increase visitors so there is no advantage to having their robot come to visit.

Some bad robots don't obey the *robots.txt* file. In this case the site can be banned by its IP address or range of addresses. This can be done through the web server's administration utility or directly in the *.htaccess* file in the case of the venerable Apache web server:

```
<Limit GET>
order allow,deny
deny from 63.241.61.*
allow from all
</Limit>
```

This should be done judiciously as you may block some real users and it puts extra load on the web server as it now has to check the client's IP address with each request.

Robots Exclusion Standard

The robot exclusion standard gives more information about the robots.txt syntax:

```
http://www.robotstxt.org/wc/norobots.html
```

S

Sandbox

The *sandbox* is a much debated Google phenomena. SEOers have noticed that new sites that have already had lots of optimization, particularly inbound-links will rank highly for a couple of weeks in Google's results pages and then disappear for months. The theory behind sandboxing is that sites should acquire links organically, sites with lots of pre-existing links may be owned by spammers with lots of domains under their control. It is believed that Google sandboxes the site for a few months to see if it is a genuine new site with worthwhile content or if it has just been established to manipulate search results.

The Freshbot can produce a similar effect. A site that is found by the Freshbot will appear in the Google index for a few days then vanish until it is picked up by the Deepbot later in the normal update cycle. The key difference with sandboxed sites is that they are pre-optimized and often have a high potential PageRank due to inbound-links. It has been suggested that sandboxed pages can be detected by adding seven nonsense exclusion terms after the target keywords in a Google query. As the nonsense terms will not appear in any page they should have no effect on the results but will in fact show the page in its pre-sandbox position.

Some observers think they have spotted a reverse sandbox effect where sites with good content but with few inbound-links get high placement in the search engine results for a couple of months. This will give searchers the opportunity to make links to the site if the content really is good. It is a bit like the bookstore's new releases shelf, if the books are popular they will make it over to the bestsellers list.

Inbound-Links

Sandboxing makes the Black Hat technique of spamming disposable domains to the top of Google a riskier and therefore more expensive proposition. It will also discourage sites that buy high PageRank links as their effect will be delayed. Other commentators think that Google is now sandboxing all new sites. They are still indexed but they will only begin to rank in results pages after a few months wait. This doesn't seem to be born out by experience; the author created a new site in October 2004 and had it ranking in the top 20 of Google results for a target keyword within one month. It could be that the sandbox is actually applied to inbound-links. The PR effect of inbound-links depending on age, IP addresses range (to detect link farms and cross linking) and other factors.

Beating the Sandbox

No one knows for sure if the Google sandbox exists, but it seems to fit the observations and experiments of many search engine optimizers. It is clear that with new domains expectations of quick results should be tempered. It may also be a good idea to get some reasonably optimized content onto a new domain as soon as possible before the full launch to overcome this initial delay. The sandbox has introduced some hysteresis into the system in order to restore a bit of sanity to Google's results.

SERPS

SERPS stands for **S**earch **E**ngine **R**esults **P**ages (or Positioning). That is the set of links returned by a search engine in response to a user query. Search engines may display different types of listing in their results, these can include:

- Search results from their index.

- Sponsored links and Content Targeted Advertising. The separation with search results is not always clear.

- Listings from human compiled directories such as Yahoo! directory and the Open Directory Project (DMOZ).

Usually 10 to 20 links are shown on each results page. Research has shown that 80% of users do not search beyond the second page of results so it is vital to rank highly for target keywords and to have a title and description that is enticing to searchers. For example Google displays the page Title then the first block of text containing the keywords. Other search engines select text from the top of the page or use the Meta Description tag.

The SERPS acronym is frequently used by people in the search engine community who may refer to the SERP (keyword and results) that they are targeting. A website's position within SERPS for a given keyword or phrase is an indicator of the success of their search engine optimization strategy.

Site Maps

A site map provides users with a means to navigate directly to content within your website. It is particularly useful where a user encounters a broken link. This may be due to a search engine or external site that is slow to update inbound-links following a change to the website. The web server can be configured to redirect any *Not Found* or *HTTP 404* errors to the site map.

Site maps have a potentially important role in search engine optimization. They overcome problems with dynamic content that some search engines have trouble navigating.

Some large websites have deep hierarchies of links. Search engines take time to traverse (spider) these hierarchies and index all the pages in a website. A site map can provide deep links to all the content on the website. For efficient indexing no content should be more than two links away from the home page. The site map should therefore link directly from this page. The map should be written in plain HTML. Leave natty animated site maps written in JavaScript, Shockwave or other technologies to deep-pocketed corporates who design their sites principally to impress the board. The site map is also another place to use relevant anchor text. Every page on the site should link to the home page, this means that every page is only a couple of clicks away from the sitemap. Search engines that find your site through a deep link now have a mechanism to explore the rest of the site.

Google advises against using more than 100 links on a page, many SEO experts suggest no more than 50 links, and against having pages of more than 100 kilobytes in length. It seems that Google will index more than 100 links but it may take repeated visits to the page. Some search engines may not spider to the end of a long page. This poses a problem for large sites. First of all the site map should be more than just a series of links. Use headings (H1, H2, H3 etc.) to divide the links into themed areas and use your topic keywords in those headings. If your site is well structured this will probably follow the existing themes. If the map grows too large, place topic areas into separate sub-maps. This increases the depth of the site map so more important links should be on the main map but it is better to add depth to the sitemap than risk search engines giving up due to the quantity of links.

Outbound-Links and Page Rank Dilution

The site map is a good place to put reciprocal link pages. These are general external links that are of use to anyone visiting the site. You may still want to include some outbound-links within your content pages, but these should be reserved for excellent and highly relevant information that complements the content.

There are two reasons for doing this. It seems logical to group a map of external and internal links. External links will go into a separate hierarchy from the site-map. This also has positive implications for PageRank dilution without resorting to sneaky tricks such as none-spiderable link pages or JavaScript cloaking. The section on PageRank showed that outbound links reduce the amount of PageRank available to the site. A site map generally has a large number of links within the site, it may have a high PageRank but this is well distributed to pages even deep within the site's hierarchy. Adding another link to a page with reciprocal links does little to upset that distribution.

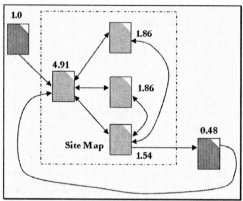

Figure 16. Site maps and PageRank dilution

Figure 16 shows this graphically. It is a small site with one inbound link and a links page with a single cross-link. If the links page had come straight from the home page the PageRank available for internal distribution would have been reduced considerably.

Site Rank

It would be nice to know how our website ranks in a search engine for a particular search term. It is quite feasible to do this by typing the keywords into a search engine and trawling through the results. However this is longwinded especially if you have a number of keywords to check. You could always write a program that accessed the search engine and sifted through the results for you. However parsing web pages is not very convenient and your program will use search engine resources that would be better used answering genuine queries. Google and other search engines specifically discourage this kind of query.

There is an alternative. Google has published a Web Service API:

```
http://www.google.com/apis/
```

This provides access to the Google search engine through third party applications. The results are delivered in a format that is easy to process. The good news is that Google allows you to use this API to create tools to check site rank etc. To use the web service you have to download the developer's kit, create a Google API account and write programs using your Google License Key. A single key enables you to make 1000 queries per day.

This still requires you to install a development environment on your computer and know a bit about programming (more later). If this is not your cup of tea there are a number of tools on the Internet that use the Google API. You'll need your own Google API key to use some of them so applying for an account is a good idea anyway.

Site Rank Tool

The following piece of code is written in the Perl computer language. Perl is a popular interpreted scripting language oriented towards the processing of text. The program accesses the Google API through the Simple Object Access Protocol (SOAP) Lite module that is part of the Perl language. If you are using Microsoft Windows you will need to download ActiveState's:

```
http://www.activestate.com
```

version of the Perl language called ActivePerl. You will also need the Google developer's kit and a Google API license key. Install ActivePerl and check that it works by opening a command line interpreter (DOS Window) and typing Perl. Save the program below to a file called: *rankme.pl*. You will need to add your license key to the file and copy another file called *GoogleSearch.wsdl* to the same directory as *rankme.pl*. This last file tells the SOAP interface how to access the Google Web Service API.

```
#!c:/usr/perl/bin/perl
# Perl client to check google site rank
#
# (c) Copyright 18 August 2004 David George
#
use SOAP::Lite;
use strict;

# uncomment this line if you access the Internet via a proxy
server
#$ENV{HTTP_proxy} = "http://localhost:80/";;

# add your own google API key here
my $key="XXXXXXXXXXXXXXXXXXXXXXXXXXXXXXXXX";

my $query = $ARGV[0] || "-h"; # either type on the command line
or it defaults to help
my $domain ="http://$ARGV[1]/";
my $max=$ARGV[2] || 100; # defaults to 100 search results

if ($query eq "-h") {
    print qq|usage:
    keyword(s) domain [max]\n
    keyword(s) - keyword to search, surround multiple keywords
with quotes
    domain - The domain to be ranked, e.g. www.google.com
    max entries - max number of results to check, higher values
take longer, defaults    to 100
    \n
    examples:
    widgets www.mywidget.com
    "widget wranglers" www.mywidget.com/wranglers 1000
    \n|;
    exit;
}

# this file must be in the same directory
my $service = SOAP::Lite
    ->service('file:GoogleSearch.wsdl');
```

```
print "rank domain $domain for keywords $query, checking $max
results\n";

my $found=0;
my $loop=0;
my $time=0;
my $total;
while ($loop < $max) {
    # $result is hash of the return structure. Each result is an
element in
    # the array keyed by 'resultElements'. See GoogleSearch.WSDL
for details.


    # results are delivered in blocks of ten
    my $result = $service->doGoogleSearch($key,
xml_clean($query), $loop, 10, "false", "", "false", "",
"latin1", "latin1");
    if ($loop==0) {
        $total=$result->{estimatedTotalResultsCount};
    }

    if(defined($result->{resultElements})) {
        my $start = 0;
        $time+=$result->{searchTime};

        while ($start < 10) {
            my $url=$result->{resultElements}->[$start]->{URL};
            $start++;
            if ($url =~ /$domain/) { # match start of url
                $found++;
                print "rank: $start $url\n";
            }
        }# while
    }
    $loop+=10;
}# while

if ($found == 0) {
    print "No entry for $domain in first $max found\n";
}
    print "Search Took: $time seconds, found: $found in a total
number of responses: $total\n";


sub xml_clean {
    my $text = shift;

    $text =~ s/\&/\&amp;/g;
    $text =~ s/</\&lt;/g;
    $text =~ s/>/\&gt;/g;
    $text =~ s/\"/\&quot;/g;
    $text =~ s/\'/\&apos;/g;

    return $text;
}
```

Examples

The following examples are for demonstration purposes only and don't represent real searches. They show how the *rankme* tool can be used to evaluate how well a page is optimized for a range of criteria.

The keywords: *search engine optimization* are used for all the examples. Google will find pages which contain these keywords in any order, although it will have a preference for the order given. To search for the exact phrase enclose it in quotes.

Keyword Search

Check first 35 results for keyword phrase *"search engine optimization"*:

```
rankme.pl "search engine optimization" www.abcseo.com 35

rank domain http://www.abcseo.com/ for keywords search engine
optimization, checking 35 results
rank: 29 http://www.abcseo.com/seo-book/
rank: 30 http://www.abcseo.com/comments/A133_0_1_0_C/
Search Took: 0.651425 seconds, found: 2 in a total number of
responses: 2970000
```

The results tell us that there are 2,970,000 results for the keywords. A competitive phase. The site: *abcseo.com* lies in 29th and 30th place.

Anchor Text Search

The same search is repeated but looking for query in the anchor text only. Google ranks all the sites that have at least one in-bound link containing this anchor text:

```
rankme.pl "allinanchor:search engine optimization"
www.abcseo.com 35

rank domain http://www.abcseo.com/ for keywords
allinanchor:search engine optimization, checking 35 results
rank: 21 http://www.abcseo.com/articles/seo/
Search Took: 0.962904 seconds, found: 1 in a total number of
responses: 90,100
```

There are 90,100 sites with this in-bound link, *abcseo.com* is number 21.

Body Text Search

The search can be restricted to just the page contents using the *intext* operator. This search ignores URLs, anchor text and document title:

```
rankme.pl "allintext:search engine optimizations"
www.abcseo.co.uk 35
rank domain http://www.abcseo.co.uk/ for keywords
allintext:search engine optimizations, checking 35 results
rank: 30 http://www.abcseo.co.uk/seo/
Search Took: 1.365586 seconds, found: 1 in a total number of
responses: 3380000
```

Title Element Search

The *title* operator restricts the search to documents where the query occurs in the title element:

```
rankme.pl "allintitle:search engine optimization" www.abcseo.com
35
rank domain http://www.abcseo.com/ for keywords
```

```
allintitle:search engine optimization, checking 35 results
rank: 21 http://www.abcseo.com/seo-book/
Search Took: 0.966249 seconds, found: 1 in a total number of
responses: 276,000
```

URL Search

The *inurl* operator restricts the search to the documents where the query occurs in the Uniform Resource Locator (URL)

```
rankme.pl "allinurl:search engine optimization" www.abcseo.co.uk
35
rank domain http://www.abcseo.co.uk/ for keywords
allinurl:search engine optimization, checking 35 results
No entry for http://www.abcseo.co.uk/ in first 35 found
Search Took: 0.828275 seconds, found: 0 in a total number of
responses: 16800
```

In this case no results were found, which is what we would expect as the term does not occur in any of the domain's web addresses.

Some Useful Google Query Operators

Google supports the following query operators

- **intitle:** Putting *intitle:<query>* in front of a query term will restrict the results to documents containing that word in the title. Put the query in quotes to search for the exact query in the title.

  Note: Putting *intitle:* in front of every word in your query is equivalent to putting *allintitle:* at the front of your query.

- **allintitle:** Starting a query with the term *allintitle:* restricts the results to those documents with *all* of the query words in the title.

- **inurl:** Putting *inurl:* in front of the query term restricts the results to those documents containing that word in the result URL.

  Note: *inurl:* only works on words and ignores punctuation, so *inurl:apple.co.uk*, will search for URLs containing the terms *apple co uk* in any order

- **allinurl:** Starting a query with the term *allinurl:* restricts the results to those documents with all of the query words in the result URL.

- **allintext:** Starting a query with the term *allintext:* restricts the results to those documents with all of the query words in the body text and ignores link, url and title matches.

- **allinlinks:** This operator no longer appears to work, see *allinanchor*.

- **allinanchor:** Starting a query with the term *allinanchor:* restricts the results to those documents that have all of the query words in their inbound-links.

For further information refer to the page:

```
http://www.google.com/help/operators.html
```

Spamming

The term *Spam* comes from a Monty Python comedy sketch set in a trucker's café. All the dishes on the menu come with spam - a type of tinned ham. In the computer world spam is used to denote excessive repetition: multiple posts, usually commercial, to forums and unsolicited email are the two most frequent examples. For SEOers the term includes the excessive use of keywords, duplicate content, unnatural link structures and the posting of links to guestbooks and membership lists.

Blog comment, guestbook and member list spam

The blog or weblog phenomena has done a great deal to revitalize interest in the Internet following the dot.com bust. Using Content Management Software blogs enable even technical neophytes (aka *newbies*) to publish their message. Blogs range from personal diaries to online-newspapers written by professional writers and journalists who enjoy the editorial freedom the medium offers.

Blogs also have two features which attract high search engine rankings. Bloggers link freely to other sites, creating dense inter-linking between highly themed content. Bloggers are also prodigious, creating large quantities of fresh content. Blogs were designed from the start to be interactive. Readers can post comments and usually include links to other sources. These features mean that the most popular blogs have PageRanks of 7.

The popularity of blogs was quickly spotted by the black-hatters. They found that they could boost the rankings of their own sites by using the comment, guestbook or member list features that are part of most blog software. Typing *blog, weblog* or *guestbook* into Google will bring up many high-ranking targets, especially when the query is combined with the *inurl* operator. Usually a spammer's comment is completely irrelevant and is posted to multiple blogs as part of the same campaign:

```
Great article about global warming, why don't you cool off a bit
check out this page on hot babes?
```

Spammers even run automated scripts known as *spambots*. These attempt to post comment spam to sites running well known blog software. The aim is quantity rather than quantity but it can mean that a single site gets hit by huge numbers of comments, often posted at the same time.

Blog spam had the advantage of keyword rich anchor text coupled with highly ranked pages. The aim is not just to get click through traffic but to subvert the ranking algorithms used by search engines. The fresh content offered by blogs means they get frequent visits from search engines. A day spent spamming the most popular blogs can rapidly boost a website to the top of the search engine results pages. As is often the case on the Web some of the most virulent spammers are pushing adult content sites and cover their tracks using anonymous proxies and compromised *zombie* hosts.

The popularity of this technique has spread rapidly and blog spammers have soon found themselves in an arms race. They have to visit the best blogs on an ever more frequent basis as other messages soon push their links off the coveted and highly ranked home page into search engine oblivion.

Needless to say blog owners are none too happy with this state of affairs. Some have removed comment pages or disabled the capability to post links. Others, wishing to preserve the spirit of the medium, spend hours moderating and removing a veritable tidal wave of spam. Technical solutions have been adopted, disguising outbound-links using JavaScript or rerouting links via a hidden page to stop anchor text and PageRank benefits from being transferred. The three main search engines, Google, Yahoo! and MSN have even proposed a new *nofollow* value to the *rel* attribute of the HTML anchor element:

```
<a href="http://www.spamsite.com/" rel="nofollow">cheap
viagra</a>
```

This tells search engine robots not to give any value to this link. The search engines hope that Content Management Software vendors will use this attribute value when generating comment links. As some comment links are genuinely useful this risks breaking a vital resource for the PageRank algorithm.

Spammers are nothing if not persistent and spam-kiddies are often unaware that their efforts now have little effect. Search for Google for:

```
Guestbook + <your keywords>
```

and you can still find many examples like this one on a basketball site:

```
Name: Penis Enlargement Pills
Web Page: http://www.online-penis-enlargement-pills.com/
Gender: Male
Comments: I just wanted to say WOW! your site is really good and
im proud to be one of your perm. surfers, be sure to my penis
enlargement pills project site, dont laugh! here is my penis
enlargement pills site: penis enlargement pills
```

It may also have the effect of intensifying spam as spambots may take an ever more scattergun approach to posting. One theory on why spammers are so poor at grammar and spelling is that it helps trick automatic (Bayesian) spam filters. I suspect that after typing in 500 spam messages in a session they just get lazy.

Referrer spam

Referrer spam shows just how ingenious black-hatters can be in finding ways to manipulate search engine rankings. When someone clicks on a hyperlink their browser opens up the new web page. As part of the communications process (called HTTP which stands for HyperText Transfer Protocol) their browser sends the web address (URL) of the page containing the hyperlink. This address is called the Referrer. The user's web server will log this address and it is useful for traffic analysis, for example to judge the effectiveness of inbound-links.

There are a number of programs for analyzing raw log-files such as AWStats and Webalizer. These produce web pages summarizing user access on a monthly basis. Unfortunately many reports are publicly accessible and indexed by search engines and with a little knowledge about their format it is possible to locate them. Searching Google for phrases that typically occur within reports such as:

```
"Generated by Webalizer" or "Created by awstats"
```

will return thousands of Webalizer and AWStats reports. It is easy to write a script to make requests to websites with fake Referrer URLs. For example using the popular cUrl tool this would be:

```
c:\ curl.exe -e http://www.mySite.com/
http://www.targetSite.com/
```

Webalizer lists the top 25 Referrer URLs in its monthly statistics. The spammer merely has to bombard the site with enough requests to figure in this chart. This creates an inbound-link, containing keywords, boosting Page or Web Rank. Some of these log pages have surprisingly high Google PageRanks.

Referrer spam has become an increasing problem. Spammers have armies of zombie hosts at their command ready to launch a campaign. These zombies are computers on the Internet where the spammer has installed a server by using some security flaw in the Operating System, usually Windows. Often a scatter gun approach is adopted, the spammer doesn't know if the log file is indexed by search engines or not and hopes that at least a percentage of the spam will make it through. Webmasters running Apache can look at the *mod_security* package as a way to combat this kind of spam by blocking popular keywords in referrer pages, examples would be: *poker, Viagra and loans.*

The technique is definitely Black Hat. It manipulates search engine rankings by creating what are in effect fake inbound links. It subverts the HTTP Referrer mechanism. It clogs log files with bogus information and it consumes resources on the target web server.

Black-hatters may counter that it is up to server administrators to protect against this form of spam but that is like saying that homeowners must lock their doors or risk being robbed. There is usually no good reason to have log-files publicly viewable. The log files should be password protected and preferably not visible to the Internet. Webmasters can also use a *robots.txt* file to stop search engines from indexing their logs. Log reports have many outbound-links on a single page so the overall benefit of each link is limited.

Keyword Spam

Keyword spam is the excessive repetition of keywords on a page. It is usually done using hidden HTML elements that are indexed by search engines but are not visible to users including Title, Meta, and Alt text. Black-hatters have found that they can disguise keywords in the contents of the page by making the text the same color as the background and tucking it away at the bottom of the page. However this still takes up space so may be noticed by competitors, particularly if they type CTRL-A to highlight all the text on a page. It is possible for search engines to detect text which is the same color as the background and this could flag that the page is using spammy techniques. MSN Search claims to automatically penalize such pages.

An extension on the hidden text idea is to hide the keyword spam using style-sheets (CSS). This gives the spammer great scope for stuffing keywords into important elements such as Headings without them being noticed. The following style will format all Heading 1 text as 1pt high white text.

```
H1 {
  font-size : 1pt;
  color : white;
}
```

There are many other ways of hiding content from users such as Layers and IFrames while still having it visible to search engines. Remember that it is possible to detect the most obvious examples of spam although forcing search engines to parse style sheets and other structures slows down indexing so few, if any, currently do this.

Reporting Spam

If you spot a competitor using obviously spammy techniques you can report them. Google and Yahoo! have web pages that let you specify the exact nature of the problem you have found.

```
Google
http://www.google.com/contact/spamreport.html

Yahoo!
http://add.yahoo.com/fast/help/us/ysearch/cgi_reportsearchspam
```

Obviously they won't ban sites where there is no contravention so don't waste time reporting all your competitors.

Stemming

Stemming is the ability to automatically search for different forms of a keyword. If the word *computers* is queried, the search engine may also return pages containing *computing, computed, computer, computation* etc. *Computer* is the stem or root word.

Yahoo! and Google support stemming by default. Google introduced stemming around the time of the Florida update leading some pundits to suggest this was the cause of the major upheavals that some highly optimized commercial sites suffered. Google's stemming algorithm provides a wider choice of results where the keywords used are too restrictive. You will notice it most on queries with three or more keywords.

Stemming means that it is no longer necessary to target different forms of a single word in optimizations. However the specific keywords will rank better than their stemmed variants.

Stop Words

Stop Words are words that are so common that they have little relevance to the context of a web page. Examples would be adverbs, conjunctions and prepositions. Excluding stop words saves resources on search engines with little effect on the quality of results.

Google uses single letters and numbers as stop words as well as the following list.

about	an	and	are	as
at	be	by	for	from
how	in	is	it	of
or	that	the	this	to
was	what	when	which	who
why	will	with		

Table 4. Stop Words

Searchers can ask search engines to include stop words by using the '+' symbol before the stop word or by putting the entire search phrase in quotes but such searches are the exception rather than the norm. They are often used where the searcher knows an exact phrase from a page. A good example is the start of Hamlet's soliloquy, *"To be or not to be, that is the question"*. The results without the stop words are very different.

Except for these specific cases stop words should be avoided in phrases that target keywords. Examples would be in Anchor Text, Title elements and ALT (alternative) text in image links. This should not be taken to extreme, for example headings should still include stop words where it helps the readability of the content.

T

Topic-Sensitive PageRank

Described at the May 2002 World Wide Web (WWW) proceedings:

```
http://www.stanford.edu/~taherh/papers/
```

Topic-Sensitive PageRank (TSPR) was developed by Taher H. Haveliwala at Stanford University, the same establishment that spawned Google. Dr Haveliwala was hired by Google in October 2003. TSPR uses search query information to influence link based scores. Unlike PageRank, an inbound-link only counts if it is deemed to be on-topic. Compared to algorithms such as Hilltop it requires minimal real-time processing and does not require a corpus of expert pages related to the search keyword(s).

Like the original Google PageRank algorithm, TSPR computes ranking scores during the indexing of web pages. However it computes multiple ranking scores with respect to various topics. In the original study the topic areas were taken from a top level category of the Open Directory Project. For example, for computing these could be:

- Artificial Intelligence
- Desktop Publishing
- Hacking
- Multimedia
- Open Source
- Operating Systems
- Programming
- Virtual Reality

Topics are more general than keywords. At query time these scores are combined relative to the search query to form a composite PageRank. As with PageRank this score is used in conjunction with other factors to produce a final ranking.

For an inbound-link to count under the TSPR algorithm the linking page's theme must be related to the query.

Traffic Analysis

Every time someone directly accesses a page on your website your server writes a line of information in a log file. If you are serious about search engine optimization these log files are mines of information that can show you which search engine robots are visiting your site, any problem pages and keywords used to find your pages.

Web server log files come in a few standard formats which means that there is a wide range of software available, both free and commercial, to read and analyze the information. Here is an example of a single entry in a log file:

```
64.203.3.83[1] - 64.203.3.83.128711091328144596
[01/Aug/2004:03:42:56 +0100][2] "GET[3] /index.htm[4] HTTP/1.1" 200[5]
15101[6] http://www.blogspot.com/widgetblog/index.htm[7] "Mozilla/4.0
(compatible; MSIE 6.0; Windows NT 5.1)"[8]
```

This shows the numeric IP address of the computer requesting the page[1], the time of the request using Greenwich Mean Time (GMT)[2], the request type[3] and file name[4]. The server HTTP error code[5]: 200 is good, 301/302 are redirects and 404 is an error caused by a broken link, the number of bytes (characters) downloaded[6], the URL of the page the user was viewing prior to this request[7] (called the referrer) and the user agent (web browser type) and operating system[8].

This entry comes from the log file of a site that I manage. Each month the site has over one million log entries. It can sometimes be useful to look at raw log files but usually an individual entry doesn't tell us a great deal. What is interesting are trends over time and for that Log File analysis software is essential.

Limitations of Log Files

Before we go further and because it is the one area where commercial packages try to add value we should discuss the limitations of log files.

As we saw above, logs show direct accesses to the server for a page. However there are lots of chances for the request to be satisfied before it ever reaches our server. In this case we will have no log entry even though the user is viewing our content. The user may already have viewed the page and his web browser will find a copy of the page directly on the hard disk in a zone known as a cache. Caching, that is storing a copy of some information close to the user, is a popular technique for speeding up access times to a slow resource - such as a web page. The page may also be cached on a proxy server run by the user's organization or Internet Service Provider. These are used to reduce outgoing traffic for frequently accessed resources. The web hosting company may also operate a special front-end cache, called an accelerator, to reduce load on its servers. Pages are kept in the cache for anything from 24 hours to a week before being refreshed. Sometimes caches are configured to check with the origin server (our website) to see if the resource has been updated without actually downloading the resource, in which case this will be counted as a request.

Accesses via a cache will mean that log files will underestimate traffic to our website. They also mean that lots of accesses will appear to come from a single computer. Remember the IP address in the log file represents a computer and not a user. Some large ISPs also host their caches across many computers each with its own address, thus a single user may have his requests split over a number of IP addresses.

The referrer information tells us which page the user was visiting immediately before requesting our page. This may be from an inbound link or search engine. In the latter case it will usually include the keywords used to find our page. The referrer information is not guaranteed to be correct and some web surfers run special software to disguise this field. The same goes for the user agent information. It is often necessary to alter this as some websites write pages for Microsoft's Internet Explorer and bar other browsers based on the user agent information, even though those browsers could view the pages. This is not really in the spirit of the Web and so surfers configure their browsers to send the same user agent information as Internet Explorer. User agent information will also tell you which search engine robots are visiting your website and the information is an integral part of creating cloaked web pages.

For simplicity the Web communications protocol (HTTP) is stateless. That means that each request is stand-alone. This is a good thing on something as potentially unreliable as the Internet where crashes to computers and communication outages occur. It does mean that it is not possible to tell if individual requests are from the same user even if the IP address information is the same. Websites that need to track users around the site use features such as cookies to tie individual requests together. A cookie is a unique piece of information that is sent to the web browser when it first connects to a site. The browser then sends this information back each time it requests a new page on the same site.

All of this means that there is no 100% accurate way of tracking a single user's access to a site via log files. The only thing that can be said with any certainty is that the website received at least the number of hits recorded in the log file. Commercial packages such as *Mach 5* and *WebTrends* give the paths that a user takes through the site. They construct this through a combination of IP address, time, referrer field and user agent. The assumption being that requests in the same time frame, say less than 30 minutes, from the same computer using the same web browser are probably from the same user. However they will not see pages accessed through the web browser back and forward buttons as these will be served by the local copy of the page. They will also miss pages fetched from the browser or other cache. There is also no way of knowing where the user went after they leave the site.

Many analysis tools also report website *stickyness*, either in terms of time spent reading the site or the number of pages read per visit. A visit is defined as a series of requests from the computer/browser combination over a certain period. The time a user spends on a page is measured as the time between two page requests by the same user. There is no certainty that the user actually spent this time reading the page. Overall time browsing the site is also inaccurate due to caching and the fact that the time on the exit page cannot be known. Print media suffers from similar, if not more serious deficiencies. A magazine publisher knows how many copies are printed, using an audit bureau they may even know how many are sold. However determining how many people see each magazine, or which articles they actually read can only be done by reader surveys. Keep these restrictions in mind, especially when listening to the claims of salesmen.

Analysis and Search Engine Optimization

Log files can be used to answer the following questions

- Whether the website is being indexed by a particular search engine robot
- What are the most popular pages on the site
- Which pages are causing problems, for example single access and exit pages
- Which missing pages are requested
- Where is the website traffic coming from - remote sites, search engines, geographic locations
- What search keywords are used to find the site

Log files are also useful for identifying hacking and spamming attempts. The timestamp information must be accurate if you wish third parties, such as ISPs, to help you.

If log files are archived for each month they can also be used to identify problems that can occur with the site and to judge the effects of advertising, link and keyword campaigns.

Robots/Spiders

Most search engine robots are configured to report a specific user agent when they visit a website. The Yahoo! robot reports:

```
Yahoo! Slurp
```

Log analysis software will translate these entries into a report that gives:

- How many robots visited the website

- How many pages they have indexed

- How much bandwidth robots have consumed

Remember that bandwidth used by spiders is overhead although it should have the benefit of later visits to the website. I have even considered banning some spiders that eat lots of site bandwidth but send few visitors but have hesitated on the grounds that today's bandwidth hog may just be tomorrow's gold mine.

If you want to know if a search engine has indexed a particular page you will have to look at the log file:

```
65.54.188.134 - 65.54.188.134.325781095131986605
[14/Sep/2004:04:19:46 +0100] "GET
/products/widgets/description.htm HTTP/1.0" 200 9303 "-"
"msnbot/0.11 (+http://search.msn.com/msnbot.htm)"

65.54.188.134 - 65.54.188.134.325781095131986605
[14/Sep/2004:04:19:53 +0100] "GET /products/widgets/order.htm
HTTP/1.0" 200 9303 "-" "msnbot/0.11
(+http://search.msn.com/msnbot.htm)"
```

This shows that version 0.11 of the MSN Search robot visited the widget description page on the 14th of September and then indexed the order page seven seconds later. The file, *order.htm* is a link from the description page. This shows that the robot is able to traverse the pages without any problems. This doesn't guarantee that the pages will make it into the index or that people will find them.

This information was obtained using the command line *grep* tool. Perl is also a great language for writing ad-hoc scripts to analyze log files. If programming isn't for you, you may be able to find someone to help with these tasks.

Page Requests

Analysis software will tell you which your most popular pages are. Usually these are home pages and other *hub* pages. It is useful to be able to filter scripts, images, style sheets and other non-content pages from this list. Some software will allow you to consolidate all requests below a hub page or within a directory tree or to produce customized reports. This gives an idea of which areas are most popular with users. Of course the lack of popularity of certain pages may be down to poor site structure, perhaps they are buried too deep, or maybe other parts of the site have better inbound-links?

Deep pages may not even get indexed by search engines. This can be confirmed by looking at the site logs. Over a reasonable period, say several months, it should be possible to identify all the pages that are indexed by a search engine robot and compare this with a list of pages for the site. A well structured site map is one solution to enable both search engines and users to find all the content on your site.

Some software can tell you which the least popular pages are. The caveat is that a page must have at least one request to feature in this list. You should also have a list of all pages on the site and include those pages with zero requests over a reasonable time frame in this list. If there are important pages on this list, for example those pages that generate revenue your site, they may need to be restructured or have the content modified.

Exit pages show the last pages that users visited. Is there a reason why users jump off at this point? Perhaps the page is a bit of a dead end with dull content and few exciting internal links to follow. Entry pages are usually those that have inbound-links, figure high in search engine results for popular keywords or are bookmarked by users. Can the same tactics that make these pages winners be applied elsewhere, in particular to hub-pages? Orphans or single access pages are pages that visitors see without exploring the site further. These should be entry pages but do not work to entice visitors further into the site. Is the content boring? Is the link structure poor?

Keep a log of the changes that are made to the site and monitor logs to see what effect these changes have.

Error Pages

If you've ever restructured a site, something to be avoided but that can happen through poor initial design choices, you will see a lot of error pages. These are entries in the log file where the server returns a *404* code to the user. They can be caused by inbound-links pointing to non-existent files or to a search engines that has not yet updated its index. In the latter case this can take several months as search engines do not automatically drop a page they can't find. The first thing to do is to redirect errors to your site map so that users can attempt to find the missing resource. Depending on the web server there are different ways of doing this. On Apache this is enabled through the *.htaccess* file:

```
ErrorDocument 404 /sitemap.htm
```

If the file has moved you may want to redirect requests to the new resource. If there are errors on script pages (in particular: *HTTP 206 - partial content delivered*) it may be that they have bugs or problems accessing resources such as databases and are timing out. You should periodically check the internal link structure and the outbound-links. A tool such as the freeware Xenu Link Sleuth:

```
http://home.snafu.de/tilman/xenulink.html
```

will automate this process. Be aware that if you pay for your website's bandwidth this can be quite expensive on resources. It is a good idea to set up a staging mirror site, to perform link and other tests before migrating the changes to the live site.

Watch out for any search engine robots that get strange error results. Your site will not get indexed if they can't see your content. Some webmasters have reported Googlebot seeing *406 - no acceptable content* errors. The Googlebot will only accept HTML and text content types but the server wants to return a different type of content.

Geographic Information

Geographic information shows where visitors are located. At its simplest, log analysis software will use the top-level domain name (TLD) such as *.uk, .fr, .com* to identify the user's location. More complex analysis uses the numeric IP address; these are assigned by coordinating bodies that allocate Internet addresses in blocks to certain geographic locations. If your website is aimed at North-American visitors then users from other countries are consuming bandwidth without necessarily adding to revenue. With something as global as the Internet incidental visitors can't be avoided but it could be that the site content and inbound-links require work.

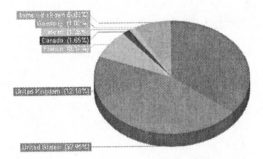

Figure 17. Geographic Locations of Visitors

Similarly if you wish to appeal to other markets then you may need to create pages in the local language and target regional search engines and directories, for example Voila for France or Google UK.

Paths

Paths show the routes visitors take through your website. Well conceived commercial sites are often built around purchase scenarios. For example a user visits the widgets entry page, reads up on widgets, maybe takes one for a virtual test and then proceeds to make an online purchase. These scenarios are story boarded by marketing departments before being translated into content by web designers and programmers.

Path analysis is a feature of a number of commercial tools and determines, within the limits of the information present in log files, the actual paths taken by users through the site. If users suddenly drop out at some point during the scenario the exit page will require work. These reports are particularly useful after a restructuring of the site or other changes that result in a drop in orders. The path to the order page can be followed to find out where potential clients are being lost.

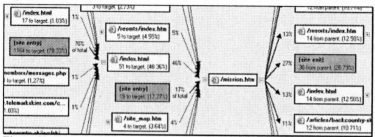

Figure 18. Usage Paths as reported by Mach5 Analyzer

Referrers

The biggest source of traffic is search engines, directories and inbound-links. The percentages in which search engines appear on your traffic report should roughly correspond to their market share. If they don't it may be worth considering optimization strategies for the search engine. There are a number of surveys of search engine use. For the US around 40% of searches pass through Google, 30% with Yahoo, 15% with MSN Search and 5% for the rest. These surveys don't always make clear where they aggregate results, for example Google powers AOL search and Yahoo! owns AllTheWeb, AltaVista and Overture. In Europe the figure for Google rises to over 70% followed by Yahoo! and MSN Search. You can find the latest information on the Search Engine Watch:

```
http://www.searchenginewatch.com/
```

With the brouhaha surrounding anchor text and PageRank it is easy to forget that inbound-links do bring traffic. Your traffic analysis software will show the top referrers. These sites may be worth cultivating further. Similarly it may be worth investigating link partners that are not sending you much, or any traffic. Is your link hidden away somewhere or has it been dropped altogether? Referrer information will also show sites that are *hotlinking*; that is sites that are linking directly to your resources: images, videos etc. Some webmasters don't object to this but others see it as bandwidth theft. If your site is hosted on Apache or Microsoft IIS you can use rewrite rules to block hotlinks. In the following example the rules redirect hotlinks to a dummy image except where the referrer is *mydomain.com*.

```
RewriteEngine On
RewriteCond %{HTTP_REFERER} !^http://(www\.)?mydomain\.com/ [NC
RewriteCond %{HTTP_REFERER} !^$
RewriteRule \.(jpe?g|gif|bmp|png)$ images/dummy.jpg [L]
```

Keywords and Phrases

Most analysis tools will report on the keywords and phrases that were used to find your site. These can be broken down by search engine. This information is useful to show how successful your site is for your target keywords and whether you need to make some special optimizations for certain search engines.

If your site ranks amongst the top ten search results for certain keywords and WordTracker and Overture show that these keywords are popular, and yet there is little or no search engine traffic, there may be a problem with the description displayed with the results. Consider modifying the Title, first Heading and sentence of the web page or update the META description tag. Sites that spam these tags can rank highly but get few click-throughs because it is evident to users from the description that they are manipulating the search results.

Again a campaign for new keywords should monitor both the increase in site rankings and the number of users finding the site using those keywords as a search engine query. The percentages arriving from each search engine should approximate to search engine usage.

AWStats

AWStats is a free log file analysis package written in the Perl programming language and designed to be installed on a web server to enable reports to be viewed remotely via a browser. This is similar to the Webalizer statistics provided by hosting companies as part of the package. AWStats can also be run from a command prompt to analyze previously downloaded log files. The program is obtained from the site:

```
http://awstats.sourceforge.net/awstats.ftp.html
```

A recent version of the Perl language must also be installed on the machine. To run from the command line open the file called: *awstats.model.conf* and, as an absolute minimum, edit the variables SiteDomain and LogFile to give the website name and the location of the log file on the hard disk:

```
LogFile="c:/Temp/mydomain.log"
SiteDomain="www.mydomain.com"
```

There is a variable for converting IP addresses found in log files to Host names using the Domain Name Service but this makes file processing extremely slow for large log files. The analysis is run with the command:

```
awstats.pl -config=model -update
```

This performs an initial analysis and creates an AWStats file for each month in the log file. It takes around 5 minutes to process a 100Mbyte log file. Running the command:

```
awstats_buildstaticpages.pl -config=model -month=09
```

will create a series of html files for the various statistics measured for a given month (09 = September). These can be viewed with a web browser. AWStats will run on any operating system that has Perl.

Analog:

```
http://analog.cx/
```

is another free analysis tool with a popular following.

Mach5 Analyzer

Mach 5 Analyzer is a commercial package available with a limited free evaluation period from the site:

```
http://www.mach5.com/
```

It is a Windows program and is simple to install. The program offers enhanced capabilities compared to the free packages including the ability to analyze the paths users take through a website. It also offers a lot of customized reporting options. WebTrends:

```
http://www.webtrends.com/
```

is another popular commercial log analysis and reporting tool.

SamSpade

If you need to get down to the nitty-gritty of individual log files SamSpade

```
http://www.samspade.org/
```

is a useful site. You may notice a lot of traffic from a certain IP address. SamSpade can look up information about the address through the Domain Name System. This may be a new search engine robot, an email address harvester or someone who is page-jacking your entire website. You can block it, either through the *robots.txt* file or using the *.htaccess* file on Apache web servers.

Summary

Your log files are often the first indicator of problems or success with your search engine optimization strategy. This requires analyzing the results as an on-going task, noting any changes and establishing the causes. It can be as worthwhile concentrating effort on areas where you are not getting results as improving already popular areas or keywords. There are a lot of things that can be done to increase traffic to a website. Log files will show which techniques bring the most returns for a given effort.

U

Uniform Resource Locators (URLs)

If you were around during the Internet gold rush or dot.com boom or whatever they called it you will remember all those IPO reports that talked about brand creation. Apparently the suits were going to corner the Internet by squatting on great, catchy domain names and then pour bizillions of venture capital and IPO dollars into building those brands. Names like Boo.com, Kozmo.com and Webvan.com. Those environmentally friendly management consultants were recycling the same ideas they'd applied to bricks-and-mortar. Having blown huge amounts of other people's money, the three examples cited are now little more than dot.compost. Sent to the great domain name registry in the sky. It appears that the suits just didn't get the Web.

Unless you are already a well known brand, building awareness of your name takes a large marketing budget. Most websites are like a shop in main-street. You need some publicity otherwise you will get little more than passing trade from link partners. That publicity is supplied by search engines. Two components that improve rankings in many search engines are relevant anchor text and inbound-links.

Domains

When people create inbound-links to your site they often use just the domain name. For example:

`asite.com` has some interesting information on maine coons

or even worse

for information on Maine Coons `click here`

That's great with search engines that treat inbound-links as a vote for the site. Google and also Yahoo! and the new MSN Search put some store on inbound-links but we are missing out on good anchor text. We can go around asking webmasters to use specific anchor text. Some will do this but many are too busy to go back over existing links.

Now let's assume our site is all about Maine Coon cats, in fact we are a Maine Coon cat breeder. A better choice of domain name might be:

```
mainecoonbreeder.com
```

or

```
maine-coon-breeder.com
```

Whether to use hyphens or not is a trade off. Link partners will often insert the spaces when writing your domain name, the advantage with hyphens is that all the major search engines already treat these as spaces. The disadvantage with hyphens is that it makes it harder to give the domain name over the telephone or radio and it is more difficult for people to remember the exact breakdown of the words if they see the domain in print or street advertising. One member of the forum *alt.internet.search-engines* has coined the term *"oral sharing"* to describe this form of transmission. If branding is important then use shorter domains. Excessive hyphening, for example

```
bargain-international-phone-calls.com
```

may even get penalized by search engines.

So now we automatically get our main target keywords mentioned in every reference to our site. We can still trade under a different name and register that domain with a redirect to our main site just in case. This also helps us use our target keywords in our page content. Some examples:-

```
welcome to Maine-Coon-Breeder.com...
```

```
Maine-Coon-Breeder.com supplies pedigree Maine Coon kittens...
```

```
Contact Maine-Coon-Breeder.com...
```

Okay, you get the idea. Don't overdo the number of references in a page or it will look like the worst kind of spam email. The only problem with this idea is if your target keywords have already been registered. There are plenty of alternative top level domains (TLDs) such as *.org*, *.net*, *.info* or even *.co.uk*, *.fr* for a geographically based site. Search engines don't really care whether you are a dot.com or not. Most domain registrars automatically list alternatives in response to a search.

The majority of sites are not based around just a couple of keywords. The use of keywords in the domain name and URL helps with search engine optimization but being an on-page factor is not that significant. However the knowledge does give us some clues about how to structure our website. It is good practice to group pages belonging to the same theme in a subdirectory and to use keywords in the resource name. An example would be a website covering sport teams. This may, amongst other sports, cover baseball:

```
teams/baseball/new-york-yankees.html
teams/baseball/boston-red-sox.html
teams/baseball/atlanta-braves.html
```

Plan the site structure with a view to future expansion and make sure spelling is correct. Fixing problems down the line can be extremely disruptive as the ranking of a page is associated with a particular URL and it may prove impossible to update all the inbound-links. We have used hyphens in the above examples. For domain names the only legal characters are 'a' to 'z' numbers and hyphens. Both Yahoo! and Microsoft's new algorithmic search engine treat hyphens and underscores as spaces. However Google only treats hyphens as spaces and for this reason underscores should be avoided.

Multiple Domain Names

Domain names are pretty cheap these days. Some SEOers register multiple domain names for various different reasons:

- cover different spellings or misspelled words
- stop competitors registering the domain
- protect various copyrights and trademarks from cyber-squatting
- secure the domain in various geographical locations
- track traffic from specific SEO efforts... (shadow domains)
- track advertising campaigns
- target different keywords

Having a site accessible through multiple domain names can also dilute SEO efforts as each domain will be treated differently by search engines. Taken to extremes they may even trigger excessive cross-linking, duplicate page or spam filters. Some black-hatters treat domain names as a disposable resource to be used during an intensive marketing campaign and then abandoned should the search engines penalize their methods. For businesses that have invested heavily in their domain and branding this is not an option.

Shadow Domains

Some SEO companies use shadow domains to market your website. This is an alternative domain name frequently under the direct control of the SEO outfit. They may explain that this is a good idea to protect your main domain from a possible site ban because they are using dubious or aggressive tactics. However when the relationship ends they may point their shadow domain at another site, stealing any transferred benefits from PageRank and anchor text. Worse, they could sell it to one of your competitors.

Domain Redirects

If you do have to make changes you can redirect the search engine to the new pages. If you are using the Apache web server and have full access to your site you can do this with the *.htaccess* file (note the dot in front of the file name, this is a hidden file on Unix although Apache works well on Windows operating system). The *.htaccess* file is found at the root of the HTML documents directory and is a text file. Be careful editing this file as small changes can have a big effect. You should always make a backup before making changes.

Redirects can be added at the end of the file. The format is the location of the redirect file relative to the *.htaccess* file (html docroot) followed by the new, full URL.

```
redirect 301 /index.htm http://www.mydomain.com/
```

Note the figure *301*, this is an HTTP (**H**yper**T**ext **T**ransfer **P**rotocol) code. It tells search engines and web browsers that something is wrong with the requested resource. In this case *301* corresponds to *moved permanently*. Error code *302 not found* should not be used as this implies a temporary redirect and the search engine will continue to index the old page. Search engines should adjust their index to use this new URL.

It is also possible to redirect a search engine by using the Meta tag redirect in the old document:

```
<meta http-equiv="REFRESH" content="0;URL=http://www.new-
domain.com/docs/new-file.htm">
```

This Meta tag should be placed in the Head part of the HTML file and any old content removed. The search engine and any users visiting the site will first download the old file. They will then immediately load the resource specified in the URL tag. PageRank will not transfer to the new page so this technique is not recommended.

There are some fairly heinous examples of the meta tag out on the World Wide Web, at least in terms of search engine optimization. Here is one I found. The international ski resort of La Plagne in the French Alps has a website at: www.laplagne.com. Most people who link to the website use this URL and consequently they have a reasonable PR5. However, at the time of writing, if you go to the site you are immediately redirected to another page: <http://www.la-plagne.com/index_hiver.html>. What they want to do is send people to different parts of the site depending on which season it is. Their webmaster uses a Meta Refresh tag located in the Body element of the home page. The consequence is that the page with all keywords and links to the rest of the site has a miserable PR2. Time to shoot the webmaster, I think.

Domain Rewriting

The *.htaccess* solution shows its limits when we have a large number of URLs to change. If these are made to a pattern we can use a URL rewriting module. We already discussed the case of database driven content where we want to disguise dynamic URLs as search engine friendly static URLs. Under Apache the module is called *mod_rewrite* and on Internet Information Server, *ISAPI Rewrite*. .Net programmers can also use the *HttpModule* package to create a bespoke rewrite engine.

A typical use of rewriting is to combine page rank. Most websites have an address of the form:

```
http://www.mydomain.com
```

In terms of the Internet name system (Domain Name Service) there is nothing significant in the prefix *www*, it is simply a computer somewhere within the *mydomain.com* domain. DNS simply translates it to a numeric Internet (IP) Address which is how data is really moved about the Internet. Your web server could just as easily be called *snafu*. A common feature of commercial web space is that the URLs

```
http://mydomain.com
```

and

```
http://www.mydomain.com
```

map to the same Internet Address and so to the same website. However search engines think in terms of URLs so these are actually two different sites as far as they are concerned. Where inbound-links target the different domains we end up by splitting the value of the links. The following lines in the *.htaccess* file will actually create a moved *301* redirect for all pages addressed as: http://mydomain.com:

```
RewriteEngine On
RewriteCond %{HTTP_HOST} ^mydomain.com
RewriteRule (.*) http://www.mydomain.com/$1 [R=301,L]
```

Pretty cool huh? You can even create separate *.htaccess* files in subdirectories if you wish to modify a branch of the directory tree.

Sometimes these rewrite rules can cause problems where there are other redirect rules in the *.htaccess* file or you may be in an environment that doesn't support rewrites. In this case it may be possible to implement redirects programmatically in Perl, PHP or even ASP files. The following example is for PHP, an extremely popular programming language for creating dynamic Web content.

```
<?
    $request = $_SERVER['REQUEST_URI'];
    $server = $_SERVER['HTTP_HOST'];

    $prefix = strtolower(substr($server,0,4));
    if ($prefix != "www.") {
        header("HTTP/1.1 301 Moved Permanently");
        header("Location: http://www.$server$request");
        exit;
    }
?>
<HTML><HEAD><TITLE>redirector</TITLE></HEAD>
<BODY>
```

```
You are at
<?
print("<h1>$server$request;</h1>");
?>
</BODY></HTML>
```

The PHP code is between the special *<?* and *?>* tags. It gets the server name and request. It then checks the first four letters of the server name having first converted them to lowercase. Remember that Internet names are case insensitive. If the name doesn't begin with *www.* it redirects the search engine to the correct name.

Domain Registering

Make sure you secure your domain name and variants before making plans about your site public. In 1995 Digital Equipment launched the AltaVista search engine without first checking that the domain was available. In truth the benefit of a unique domain for their project probably didn't occur to them at the time. It took five years, a court case and $3.3 million before they finally secured *AltaVista.com*.

Even more flagrant was British Telecom's project to re-brand its prestigious UK research labs at Martlesham Heath. The site was to be renamed *Adastral Park*, an allusion to the fact the labs were built on a former Royal Air Force base and that the 4000 geeks housed there should themselves be reaching for the stars (the RAF's motto). Unfortunately the high powered management team had not registered the domain. A quick thinking BT contractor called Ric Hayman registered *www.adastralpark.com*, he later offered it back to BT for £2 million.

Validation

Web pages are written in the HTML or XHTML language. Like any language there are certain ground rules or standards. The process of testing a page against these standards is called *validation*. The HTML standards are defined by the World Wide Web consortium <http://www.w3c.org/>. Standards help web authors write pages that can be used by a variety of different browsers: *Internet Explorer, Firefox, Safari* or even *Lynx*. Despite these rules the world of HTML seems somewhat anarchic. This sentiment stems from the browser wars of the mid 90s when Netscape and Microsoft added new features to HTML with scant regard for existing standards. There is a feeling among some SEOers that validation is not important for search engine ranking and there is some truth in this. Point enough inbound-links at a junk page with good anchor text and Google will probably end up returning that page at the top its results. This feeling is reinforced by statement from Google:

> *"Any parser which is designed to run on the entire Web must handle a huge array of possible errors. These range from typos in HTML tags to kilobytes of zeros in the middle of a tag, non-ASCII characters, HTML tags nested hundreds deep, and a great variety of other errors that challenge anyone's imagination to come up with equally creative ones."*

In other words, forget standards, our search engine will sort out your HTML spaghetti whatever.

Benefits to Optimizers

While this may have been true when Google relied heavily on its PageRank algorithm it certainly won't prove true as search engines move into better understanding of the semantics of a page. It is easy for some web authors to forget that HTML is not a formatting but a mark-up language. It describes the structure of the document in terms of its semantic elements: Title, Heading levels, Lists, Quotations etc. While these are on-page items and therefore prone to manipulation they still give the search engine clues to the meaning of the page. Even worse, syntax errors with HTML tags may cause the search engine to confuse content and mark-up or to give the wrong significance to parts of the page.

In order to use a validation tool to trap errors the first thing to decide is which standard you are going to follow. The most popular, partially because it is the most flexible, is *4.01 Transitional*. Add a *Doctype* element at the start of each page to tell your clients, web browsers, validation and other tools and potentially robots (although they almost certainly don't use this information) that you are following this standard:

```
<!DOCTYPE HTML PUBLIC "-//W3C//DTD HTML 4.01 Transitional//EN">
```

Some web authoring tools do this for you. Once your page is online you can go the W3C's validator at:

```
http://validator.w3.org/
```

and enter the address of your page. A common error is missing ALT text from images although some web authoring tools produce very poor code.

Apart from indicating to search engine algorithms the structure of your page, validated HTML is easier for third parties such as web design companies and search engine optimization consultants to work with. It will also make the code more portable between different web authoring packages.

Although many sites rank well without adhering to standards, validation should help protect your site from changes to the way browsers and search engines work. Certainly if you are optimizing code professionally it should adhere to one of the standards.

On a related topic some web developers and optimizers like to get an idea of how their snazzy page will render on simple browsers. If validated HTML is used along with style sheets for formatting, graphically interesting pages shouldn't present any problems. Lynx is often used for this purpose as it is a text only web browser. If you don't want to install Lynx the following website:

```
http://www.delorie.com/web/lynxview.html
```

aims to emulate the output and gives a useful idea of whether the content is readable or not.

Web Authoring Tools

Web authoring tools can be the bain of an optimizer's life. Many people launch into building their website, producing lots of nice looking pages but without really understanding how the Web and in particular, search engines, work. Professional web designers are not necessarily any better, concentrating on form over function. This is why many search engine optimizers are able to beat big professional websites with multi-million dollar budgets in search engine results pages.

The HyperText Markup Language (HTML) is the basis of web pages. It is important to remember that people may want to view your content using different browsers running on various types of computer. HTML is a fairly elegant solution to this problem. The author uses special tags to identify the structure of the page: the Title, different Headings etc and then leaves it up to the user's browser to display or render this as best it can. HTML is not designed to be a WYSIWYG desk top publishing solution.

```
<DOCTYPE ...>
<HEAD>
    <TITLE>main keywords here</TITLE>
    <link rel="stylesheet" type="text/css" href="style.css">
</HEAD>
<BODY>
    <H1>main keywords here</H1>
            content...
        <H2>secondary keywords</H2>
            more related content...
        <H2>more secondary keywords</H2>
            <H3>tertiary keywords etc.</H3>
        <H2>more secondary keywords</H2>
</BODY>
```

Unfortunately there are people who don't understand this distinction. They want their pages to display exactly as they see them in their web authoring tool. As a consequence many tool designers cater for this demand. In an effort to produce WYSIWYG pages the tool generates dozens of nested tables with specific dimensions. It may insert fonts and font size information without knowing if these fonts are available to the reader's browser. Worse, it can use hidden images to try and position the various elements. Many authoring tools produce code that will not validate against any of the current standards and some produce serious errors. Microsoft Visual Studio was known to remove closing tags from HTML elements and this could cause incorrect formatting on some browsers.

All this creates a mess of HTML code. Although search engine robots are pretty tolerant about what they will accept the page will be far from optimal with a high code to content ratio. The pages may even be too long to get fully indexed, or it may take a number of passes before all the content and links are explored. The pages are also harder to optimize as the structure will be unclear. The code may also be impossible to load into a different web authoring tool.

Some web authors don't do themselves any favors when creating content, misusing mark-up elements to create particular formatting effects. They may also use formats which search engines find hard to index such as Flash animations and JavaScript driven menus. JavaScript menus are a good way of stopping search engine robots dead on your first page. If you do use JavaScript elsewhere, perhaps for validating input to forms, move the code to external JavaScript (.js) files away from the eyes of search engine robots.

Cascading Style Sheets

Cascading Style Sheets (CSS):

```
http://www.w3.org/Style/CSS/
```

were designed to address the demands of websites for better control over formatting. They enable fonts and font sizes to be customized for any HTML tag and also permit absolute positioning of elements on a page. They can also replace natty animated JavaScript menu systems with search engine friendly links and anchor text. The great thing is that all of this information can be contained in one or more external files so that web pages return to their origins: succinct mark-up and content. From the web author's viewpoint the look and feel of the whole site can be altered by changing a single file, from the robot's viewpoint the page is smaller and the intent of the mark-up usually clearer. What's more, most web authoring tools work with style sheets so there is no need to learn a complete new package. Authoring tools can often be configured to only produce code that corresponds to one of the current XHTML or HTML standards. The authoring tool may still leave a number of artifacts in the code such as unnecessary Meta information but this can be cleaned up later by a Perl script for people who are very picky.

X (Cross) Linking and Link Exchanges

Cross Linking is a popular technique designed to build traffic and increase PageRank. It relies on two websites agreeing to point an outbound-link to the other site. Many website owners spend a great deal of time exchanging links in this way and it is certainly a good way of initially getting yourself indexed by search engines and, if done correctly, getting some good anchor text.

Be careful about unsolicited emails, these can be quite friendly and chatty saying how they have found your site and you are the ideal link partner for them. Check their site out, if they are complementary to your content it may well be worth setting up reciprocal links with them. The key is equability; the website should offer you something, a strongly themed and relevant link page, good anchor text or PageRank.

Beware of professionals who want a link from your highly ranked page and will try to give little in return by using some down and dirty trickery, more of this later. Don't link to link farms. As a general rule don't link to sites with no relevance to your own and make sure their link page is actually indexed by the search engines (check the Google and Yahoo! caches). As search engines improve their algorithms, relevance and links to and from authority sites will increase in importance. You should examine the proposed link-page and home page of the site. If they have zero-page rank is this due to a ban by the search engine or is the site brand new and not yet indexed? Never link to a banned site.

Finding potential link partners is not too difficult. Go to one of the major search engines and look for sites that match your target keywords or check the link partners of your competitors (use the *link* operator in Yahoo!). Most of your direct competitors will probably not want to link with you (if they do then so much the better) so from the remainder see if they have good PageRank and a links page. You can now write to the webmasters of these sites asking for a reciprocal link. If there is no email address try *webmaster@domain* or *info@domain*. You should write a standard letter telling them about your site and why you think you complement each other. Some people even place an outbound URL before contacting the site. In any case give the URL of your links page or the page where you propose placing the link. Remember that anchor text carries weight with the major search engines so give them the exact phrase you would like in your link. Some webmasters may refuse to link to you because you have a low or even zero PageRank as reported by the Google toolbar, don't be discouraged, point out the benefits of keyword rich anchor text from a relevant page.

Cross Links and PageRank

The effect on PageRank, which is a Google concept, is more debatable. If you refer to the examples in the PageRank section you will see that the effect of adding a link to an external page boosts the PageRank of that page but dilutes PageRank available to the rest of the site.

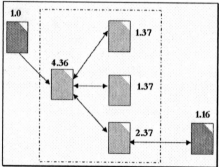

Figure 19. PageRank on cross linked site

Figure 19 is a very simple example of the effect of adding an external link, compare this with figure 11 on page 90.

Assuming the Google toolbar is reliable (it can go a while before being updated) each PR value is worth around 8 times the previous level. Thus a link from a PR 5 page is worth 64 times that from a PR3 page. At the same time you need to divide the number of outbound-links on the page to gauge the PageRank benefit to your site.

Link Campaigns and Reciprocal Link Management Tools

Running a successful link exchange campaign takes a lot of time and organization. There are a number of free and commercial link management tools that help to manage your reciprocal links automatically. The most common features include:

- users initiated link requests

- administration features to check and approve the request, this may include showing the ranking of the user's page etc.

- monitoring the inbound-link with automated removal of sneaky linkers

- generation of customized search engine friendly link pages

- requesting reciprocal links from webmasters

- customized email templates

The higher end tools can be especially useful for SEOers who are managing a number of link building campaigns.

Dirty Tricks of the Cross Linkers

Many webmasters know that outbound-links dilute their site's PageRank. A lot of folks are so obsessed with Google's Toolbar and its PageRank display that they will do anything to avoid giving *"their PageRank"* away while at the same time trying to build their own high PageRank inbound-links. As we discussed on the PageRank section, dilution is a real effect but PageRank is also a less important part of the overall Google ranking process than it was.

Some webmasters disguise their outbound-links with JavaScript. These look and work okay to someone checking the page. The assumption is that search engines don't read JavaScript so they don't transfer PageRank or anchor text weighting.

```
<a href="java script:void" onclick
="window.open('http://www.some-domain.com'); return
false;">Keywords</a>

<script language="javascript" type="text/javascript">
document.write("<A HREF='http://www.some-domain.com'
target='main'>keywords</A>");
</script>
```

Another trick is to re-route outbound-links via a page that has no PageRank. This is done by placing the re-routing script in a directory protected by a *robots.txt* file. There are some good reasons to do this, such as protecting comments from blog-spam. Google does this with outbound links from its weblog site. The zero PageRank script takes the target URL as a parameter and redirects the user to the page:

```
http://www.google.com/url?sa=D&q=http://www.abcseo.com/
```

The *robots.txt* file instructs search engine robots not to index the contents of the directory containing the script. Variations on this theme are to

- directly protect any links page with robots.txt

- place links on pages with HTML Frame elements

- use an orphaned page with no inbound-links

- using the new HTML anchor *nofollow* modifier in cross-links.

Some webmasters are more worried about losing traffic than PageRank transfer and disguise the actual links using a single-pixel image or invisible text. These links show up when you look for backlinks in the search engine but are invisible to users. Of course the easiest trick is simply to *forget* to put up your inbound-link or to remove it a short time later. These tactics rely on link partners assuming people are honest and not checking their inbound-links.

Y

Yahoo!

Yahoo! began life in a campus trailer. David Filo and Jerry Yang, grad-students in Electrical Engineering at Stanford University started their guide in February 1994 to keep track of interesting sites on the Internet. Soon their list was so long it had to be divided into categories then sub-categories. The Yahoo! directory was born. Originally known by the catchy name of *Jerry's Guide to the World Wide Web*, it was later changed to Yahoo after a trawl through a dictionary. Yahoos were a brutish tribe in Jonathan Swift's tales of Gulliver's Travels. Yahoo! is said to be an acronym for *Yet Another Hierarchical Officious Oracle*.

Yahoo! was seeing millions hits by the fall of 1994 and began to attract commercial interest. In March 1995 the business was incorporated and received $2million investment from Sequoia Capital. Yahoo! got in on the first wave of the *dot.com* craze, launching its IPO in April 1996. Yahoo! shares opened at $13 and lifted to $33 on the day.

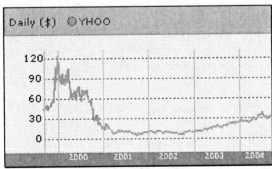

Figure 20. Yahoo's Highs and Lows

By the height of the *dot.com* boom Yahoo! was trading at over $120 a share. Boosted by online advertising revenues and the craze for Portals, then the next big thing. The tech-stock crash hit Yahoo's advertising revenues hard. By 2002 shares could be had for IPO prices.

As part of its portal strategy Yahoo! initially licensed Inktomi's search technology until replacing it in June 2000 with Google. In the summer of 2002 Yahoo! chose to merely extend its contract with Google rather than renew it.

The company was worried that Google was encroaching onto its turf as a Portal with the launch of new services such as News. From the end of 2002 Yahoo! began to acquire a number of interesting search engine technologies through the takeover of competitors including Inktomi and Overture (which already owned FAST, AltaVista and AlltheWeb). Perhaps more importantly, Overture provided Yahoo! with its patented Context Targeted Advertising technology.

These developments culminated with Yahoo! dropping Google in February 2004 and switching to its own Overture/Inktomi search engine. Clients of Google's context sensitive advertising technology (AdWords) saw no change as Yahoo! already used Overture for this service. During 2004 Inktomi also supplied results to Microsoft (MSN) Search. Estimates now give Yahoo! around 40% of the search engine traffic but this will be temporary as Microsoft is replacing Inktomi from 2005 with its own search engine technology. Currently in beta trial this will form an integrated part of Microsoft's Longhorn operating system scheduled for release in 2006.

The Overture patent also provided Yahoo! with a windfall in the form of 2.7 million Google shares prior to Google's IPO. Overture had sued Google for infringing on its patent for the auctioning of context sensitive advertising.

Yahoo! claims over 200 million visitors per month and features 25 international sites in 13 languages but faces strong competition from Google and Microsoft. Yahoo! has recently bought Oddpost and Stata Labs which it hopes will help it compete in what is seen as the next big thing: desktop search.

Optimization Specifics for Yahoo!

Before Yahoo! switched to its Overture/Inktomi search engine in February 2004 optimizing for Google also had the benefit of optimizing for Yahoo! With its new search engine Yahoo! favors on-page optimizations. Keywords in Titles and Uniform Resource Locators as well as keyword density in body text. Like Google, Yahoo offers a couple of query operators for exploring the search results:

- intitle - search for keywords in the title only
- inurl   - search for keywords in the URL

Some weight is still attached to inbound-links. Recently Yahoo! previewed a toolbar with their version of Google's PageRank, called Web Rank. This is apparently related to inbound-links although not using Google's famous, and patented, formula. Good keywords in anchor text are also a factor. If you don't have the version of the toolbar with Web Rank, Digital Point Solutions offer a Web Rank tool.

In conclusion, produce good keyword rich content for Yahoo! and concentrate on inbound-links for Google, these will also benefit Yahoo! results. Yahoo! also runs its own blog:

```
http://www.ysearchblog.com/
```
This has some general search engine buzz and information about features of
Yahoo! search.

Z

Zero Page Rank (PR0)

Webmasters using the Google toolbar will sometimes see that they have pages that have a PageRank of zero (PR0). This can cause much consternation, especially where the page has inbound-links with good PageRank and where the page itself previously had good PageRank. It is even worse when it is the home page of the website.

It generally takes a couple of crawls and some good inbound-links before a page acquires enough ranking to show on the toolbar. Toolbar PageRank can also be erratic and updates infrequent. The real PageRank may have changed a number of times before this gets reflected in the Toolbar's 0 to 10 scale.

A site that had a good PageRank that then suddenly drops to zero may indicate that it has been banned by Google for using Black Hat optimization techniques. PR0 bans manifest themselves in different ways. Sometimes the PageRank from most of the pages vanishes immediately, sometimes the PageRank drops from the home page and the ban slowly ripples through the site over a couple of updates.

The main techniques that have caused PR0 punishments are Link Farming, Jump or Doorway Pages, Hidden Content and Link Spamming through Blogs and Guestbooks. It seems that PR0 punishments are used so that the pages actually remain in the index rather than being removed entirely as happens to the most serious offenders. It is possible to recover from a ban by removing the offending optimizations and then contacting Google but this is far from guaranteed.

Some SEOers advise against cross-linking with sites that have a PR0 on the grounds that the contagion may spread to your pages. A PR0 backlink will not be worth much, except perhaps for some good anchor text although even this will have limited value from a PR0 page. Secondly the site may have a PR0 due to the aforementioned Google filters designed to detect Black Hat SEO techniques and your linked site may get banned too. Unless your domain name is disposable and you already wear a black hat don't link with any site that appears to be using these techniques to influence Google site rankings even if they still have good PR. Of course this doesn't apply to new sites with good content and with a long term potential to grow its PageRank.

Finally pages that are deep within a site may never acquire enough PageRank to show on the toolbar. This may be remedied by restructuring the internal links or adding a site map.

Endnote

You may be wondering why I'm letting you in on all these optimization secrets instead of making millions on my own website. It is a good question, and one you should ask anyone who is selling you some quick remedy to your search engine optimization woes.

To set your mind at ease I currently run a site that pays my bills through advertising. I am a techy at heart, not a businessman. I have been working on Internet related technology for nearly 20 years. I wrote one of the first Web books (Go Web! ISBN: 1850322511) back in 1995. The technical side of things is what I do well. A few years ago I started a winter sport related website, this had shed loads of great content but was pushed out of search engine rankings by sites, which I felt, didn't merit being there. Life is unfair, so I decided to fight back by studying what makes search engine's tick. This book summarizes much of what I have learned. My SEO efforts have increased the traffic to my website five fold in barely a year, it is now one of the most popular sites in its field and regularly features in the mainstream press. It also means I no longer have a boss breathing down my neck and have been able to spend the three months I researched and wrote this book in the company of my lovely baby son and his adorable mum.

Throughout this book I've tried to avoid giving you stock solutions. Instead we've concentrated on building a toolbox that will enable you to investigate, analyze and improve your search engine optimization strategies.

I don't guarantee to make you a millionaire but I will guarantee that you will vastly increase the number and quality of visitors to your website. What you do with those visitors is up to you, that is your domain of expertise.

I've advised a lot of people how to make their websites more SEO friendly. Some common problems have emerged. When you begin optimizing a website remember the KISS rule: keep it simple and stupid. Don't look for complicated solutions. A typical example is why a page cannot be found in the Google index? Website owners will search for silver bullets on the Web and often come across an array of conflicting advice, particularly in SEO forums. Search engine optimization is like the new Day Trading and these forums have a range of more, and often less, knowledgeable folk exchanging tips and remedies. Maybe the page isn't in Google because of the famous Sandbox? Or perhaps it has been banned? Although either of these may be correct they don't offer much help and can lead you up and down the garden path. If you have followed the advice in this book you will be able to investigate the problem yourself:

- Has the Google robot visited the page?

- Were there any errors reported when the page was accessed?

- Is there at least one inbound links?

- Are the link pages in the Google index?

- Did you submit the site?

Another frequent question is why site X ranks so much better than site Y? Investigate what makes site X special:

- quantity and quality of inbound-links

- anchor text

- amount of content

- freshness of content

- on-page optimizations

Maybe the site has just been around for a long time.

Search engine optimization is detective work and as the greatest detective of them all, Sherlock Holmes, once said: *"When you have eliminated the impossible, whatever remains, however improbable, must be the truth."*

Appendix I - SEO Websites and Discussion Forums

SEO FAQ

Search Engine Optimization Frequently Asked Questions. The section on search engine reverse engineering attempts to answer the question of which parts of a site are important to search engine algorithms.

```
http://www.internet-search-engines-faq.com/
```

Google Hacks

Research Buzz is the blog of the excellent Google Hack's book from O'Reilly.

```
http://www.researchbuzz.com/
```

alt.internet.search-engines

This is an Internet group for discussing all things search engine related. Not a forum as such, it is based on the Usenet distributed news network which dates from the late 1970s. If you don't have a News client you can access the group through the Google Groups interface:

```
http://groups.google.com/groups?q=alt.internet.search-engines
```

SEO Chat

SEO Chat has a huge number of forums related to all things search including separate optimization forums for each of the major search engines.

```
http://www.seochat.com/
```

Search Engine Watch

Offers tips and information about searching the Web, analysis of the search engine industry and help to site owners trying to improve their ability to be found in search engines.

```
http://searchenginewatch.com/
```

Webmaster World

Amongst other things Webmaster World discusses the promotion and marketing of a website. It offers a forum for the members to share and gain knowledge in operating and promoting a website.

```
http://www.webmasterworld.com/
```

Netiquette

When using the discussion groups mentioned you need to observe some basic standards, usually referred to as *netiquette*. Before asking a question use the search facility of the forum or even your favorite search engine to see if your question has already been asked, and answered. Don't just plunge in to a group without reading some of the conversations and getting a feel for the place and don't feed the *Trolls*. Every forum seems to have its share of Trolls, people who post inflammatory statements and enjoy senseless arguments and point scoring. SEO is not an exact science and there are many different strands of opinion. Learn and contribute and the forums will be your friend.

Appendix II: The Google API

The Google Web Service API

```
http://www.google.com/apis/
```

enables programmers to query more than 8 billion web pages from their own computer programs. The Google Web Service is built on standard SOAP and WSDL interfaces so can be accessed from a wide range of technology. Search Engine Optimizers have developed a number of useful programs using the technology. In the section on Site Rank we built a program using the PERL programming language that gives a website's position in the Google SERPs for a given set of keywords.

Web Service Interface

The following table describes the parameters to the Google Web Service interface:

Name	Description
key	Provided by Google and required to access the Google service.
q	Query Terms (see below)
start	Zero-based index of the first desired result.
maxResults	Number of results desired per query. The maximum value per query is 10.
filter	Hides very similar results and results that all come from the same Web host.
restricts	Restricts the search to a subset of the Google Web index. This could be useful if you are targeting a particular market, see Google API interface for more details
safeSearch	Enables filtering of adult content in the search results.
lr	Language Restrict - Restricts the search to documents within one or more languages.
ie	Input Encoding - no longer used
oe	Output Encoding - no longer used

Appendix III: Tools

The following tools are useful for optimizing websites.

Keyword Suggestions

This is a convenient tool that is a front end to the Wordtracker and Overture keyword databases and will show how often people search for keywords as well as proposing alternative, similar keywords.

```
http://www.digitalpoint.com/tools/suggestion/
```

PageRank Search

PageRank Search lets you query Google. The search results include a graphical representation of each site's toolbar PageRank. Remember that this value is only representative of the real PageRank Google gives a site and is just one component of Google's algorithm. It does give a guide as to how many inbound-links a site has.

```
http://www.seochat.com/seo-tools/pagerank-search
```

Keyword Analysis

This is a fantastic tool that will take your site and target keyword(s) and show how it stacks up against the top ten in terms of inbound-links, anchor text keywords, Google PageRank and overall content. It gives you an idea of what you need to do to get an important top ten position for the query.

```
http://www.mcdar.net/KeywordTool/keywordtool.asp
```

SERPS Tool

Check your SERPS (Search Engine Results Position) on Yahoo, Google, AllTheWeb. MSN and Hotbot for any given keywords to a depth of up to 10 pages of results.

```
http://www.seo-guy.com/seo-tools/se-pos.php
```

Keyword and Backlink Tracking

You will need a Google API key to use this tool. The keyword tracker lets you monitor your target keywords to see your current position. It also shows your daily, weekly and monthly change. The tool is very useful if you are running a keyword campaign and will also alert you to any search engine positioning problems on your website. You can produce customized graphs of your keyword performance.

The backlink tracker monitors a site's Google PageRank, number of inbound-links and the total number of pages indexed by Google.

```
http://www.digitalpoint.com/tools/keywords/
```

Note that the Google API has a limit of 1000 uses per key per day.

Google AdSense

AdSense Charts produces eight different types of charts for Google AdSense users. You simply have to export your Google AdSense data in CSV (comma separated variable) format.

- Impressions

- Impressions (Cumulative)

- Clicks

- Clicks (Cumulative)

- Clickthrough Percentage

- Earnings

- Earnings (Cumulative)

- Earnings Per Click

```
http://www.digitalpoint.com/tools/adsense-charts/
```

Remember that Google AdSense participants are not allowed to share their data.

The Google AdSense Sandbox shows the Google AdSense links that will be displayed on a page.

```
http://www.digitalpoint.com/tools/adsense-sandbox/
```

Bulk PageRank Checker

Displays the Google Toolbar PageRank of up to 40 URLs in one go. No need to install the toolbar.

```
http://www.top25web.com/pagerank.php
```

cUrl

Command Line URL. This tool lets you fetch the text of a web page from a command line. It is a very useful utility as it gives you complete control over the information sent to a web server and lets you examine both the returned content and headers.

```
http://www.webconfs.com/http-header-check.php
```

Perl

Practical Extraction and Reporting Language. A fast scripting language that is very useful for text processing. It is often used for programming on Web Servers.

```
http://www.perl.com
```

Active State have ported PERL to the Windows operation system:

```
http://www.activestate.com/
```

Xenu Link Sleuth

Xenu link sleuth is a free utility for checking links on a website.

```
http://home.snafu.de/tilman/xenulink.html
```

AWStats

AWStats is a free log file analyzer.

```
http://awstats.sourceforge.net/awstats.ftp.html
```

Mach5 Analyzer

Mach5 Analyzer is a commercial log files analyzer with many advanced features such as the ability to follow paths through a website.

```
http://www.mach5.com/
```

Googledance Tool

McDar's Googledance tool will show when Google's monthly dance is taking place. It has been updated for the recent changes to Google's data centers.

```
http://www.mcdar.net/dance/index.php
```

NewsFeed Software

To integrate a news feed into a website you need a server or web hosting package that supports scripting and a software package. The following are three examples.

CaRP

Supports RSS formats, written in PHP.

```
http://www.geckotribe.com/rss/
```

MagpieRSS

Supports both RSS and Atom feeds, written in PHP.

```
http://magpierss.sourceforge.net/
```

KwRSS

Kattanweb kwRSS enables RSS newsfeeds to be integrated into a website hosted on Microsoft's Internet Information Server.

```
http://www.kattanweb.com/webdev/projects/index.asp?ID=7
```

Copyscape

Given a URL Copyscape will show any duplicates on the Web.

```
http://www.copyscape.com/
```

SamSpade

SamSpade is a front end for a number of Internet tools that return information about IP addresses and domain names.

```
http://www.samspade.org/
```

Red Hat Cygwin

The Red Hat Cygwin toolset

```
http://cygwin.redhat.com/
```

is an emulation of the powerful command lines tools found on Unix (GNU Linux) operating systems. Individual commands can be built into chains to perform powerful text processing functions. They are useful for analyzing web server log files.

grep

Grep searches a file for lines matching a pattern. Patterns can be a single word, a quoted string or can use regular expressions. Regular expressions are a powerful fuzzy matching syntax. By default grep prints the matching lines.

cut

Print selected parts of line; it can be used to extract columns of information.

sort

Sorts input lines into alphabetical order and prints them to output.

uniq

Removes duplicate lines in a sorted list.

HTML Validation

HTML Pages can be validated using the W3C online tool.

```
http://validator.w3.org/
```

Printed in the United States
60599LVS00004B/144